CW01506501

Kirsten Dierolf
Solution-Focused Team Coaching

# Solution-Focused Team Coaching

by Kirsten Dierolf

Solutions
Academy

We have tried to identify all copyrights regarding the content of this book and have received permission from copyright holders. We want to thank Ben Furman, Daniel Meier, Peter Röhrig, Christian Mühldorfer, Matthias Varga von Kibéd, Insa Sparrer, Fredrike Bannink and Peter Szabo for permission to use their content

Kirsten Dierolf has asserted that she is the author of this work.

© 2014 SolutionsAcademy Verlag
Translated from the German: "Lösungsfokussiertes Teamcoaching"
SolutionsAcademy Verlag, 2013 by Kirsten Dierolf
Cover design by Kay Fretwurst, Freienbrink
Printed by BoD – Books on Demand
Printed in Germany
ISBN 978-3-944293-06-6

*For Niklas, Kai, Maxi und Jakob –*
*may you always be able to work in great teams!*

# Table of contents

Foreword by Dr Mark McKergow .......................... 11

Acknowledgements ...................................... 13

Introduction .......................................... 15

Foundations of Solution-Focused Team Coaching ............... 17

Solution-focused team coaching approaches ................... 17

If it isn't broken, don't fix it ............................ 18

If it works, do more of it .............................. 19

If it's not working, do something different ................... 20

Small steps can lead to big changes ........................ 25

The solution is not necessarily directly related
to the problem ...................................... 28

The language for solution development is different
from that needed to describe a problem .................... 32

No problem happens all the time; there are always exceptions
that can be utilized .................................. 33

The future is both created and negotiable ................... 35

Differences to individual coaching ......................... 39

Introduction ........................................ 39

Multipartiality ...................................... 42

Listening .......................................... 45

Using the language of your clients ........................ 46

Summary .......................................... 47

**Tools** . . . . . . . . . . . . . . . . . . . . . . . . . . . . . . . . . . . . . . . . . . . . . . . . . . . .  **48**

    Good working relationship . . . . . . . . . . . . . . . . . . . . . . . . . . . . . . .  48

    Pre-session Change . . . . . . . . . . . . . . . . . . . . . . . . . . . . . . . . . . . . . .  50

    Goal setting . . . . . . . . . . . . . . . . . . . . . . . . . . . . . . . . . . . . . . . . . . . .  53

    Coping questions . . . . . . . . . . . . . . . . . . . . . . . . . . . . . . . . . . . . . . . .  58

    Scaling questions . . . . . . . . . . . . . . . . . . . . . . . . . . . . . . . . . . . . . . . .  61

    Exceptions and resources . . . . . . . . . . . . . . . . . . . . . . . . . . . . . . . . .  66

    Miracle question . . . . . . . . . . . . . . . . . . . . . . . . . . . . . . . . . . . . . . . . .  68

    Small steps . . . . . . . . . . . . . . . . . . . . . . . . . . . . . . . . . . . . . . . . . . . . .  77

    Confidence, benefits and appreciative feedback . . . . . . . . . . . . . . . .  81

    Other workshop formats . . . . . . . . . . . . . . . . . . . . . . . . . . . . . . . . . .  85

    Summary . . . . . . . . . . . . . . . . . . . . . . . . . . . . . . . . . . . . . . . . . . . . . . .  94

**Team coaching processes** . . . . . . . . . . . . . . . . . . . . . . . . . . . . . . . . . . . .  **96**

    A simple process . . . . . . . . . . . . . . . . . . . . . . . . . . . . . . . . . . . . . . . . .  96

    Contract clarification . . . . . . . . . . . . . . . . . . . . . . . . . . . . . . . . . . . . .  96

    Other processes . . . . . . . . . . . . . . . . . . . . . . . . . . . . . . . . . . . . . . . . .  116

**Possible Difficulties** . . . . . . . . . . . . . . . . . . . . . . . . . . . . . . . . . . . . . . . . .  **137**

    Dealing with difficult participants . . . . . . . . . . . . . . . . . . . . . . . . . .  137

    Other possible difficulties . . . . . . . . . . . . . . . . . . . . . . . . . . . . . . . . .  143

    Summary . . . . . . . . . . . . . . . . . . . . . . . . . . . . . . . . . . . . . . . . . . . . . . .  154

**Typical requests for team coaching** . . . . . . . . . . . . . . . . . . . . . . . . . . . .  **155**

    Conflict . . . . . . . . . . . . . . . . . . . . . . . . . . . . . . . . . . . . . . . . . . . . . . . . .  155

    Bullying / Mobbing . . . . . . . . . . . . . . . . . . . . . . . . . . . . . . . . . . . . . . .  165

    Teambuilding . . . . . . . . . . . . . . . . . . . . . . . . . . . . . . . . . . . . . . . . . . . .  169

    Virtual teams . . . . . . . . . . . . . . . . . . . . . . . . . . . . . . . . . . . . . . . . . . . .  173

    Summary . . . . . . . . . . . . . . . . . . . . . . . . . . . . . . . . . . . . . . . . . . . . . . .  182

Postscript . . . . . . . . . . . . . . . . . . . . . . . . . . . . . . . . . . . . . . . . . . . . 184

References . . . . . . . . . . . . . . . . . . . . . . . . . . . . . . . . . . . . . . . . . . . . 185

Index . . . . . . . . . . . . . . . . . . . . . . . . . . . . . . . . . . . . . . . . . . . . . . . 187

List of Examples . . . . . . . . . . . . . . . . . . . . . . . . . . . . . . . . . . . . . . 189

List of Exercises . . . . . . . . . . . . . . . . . . . . . . . . . . . . . . . . . . . . . . 190

Kirsten Dierolf . . . . . . . . . . . . . . . . . . . . . . . . . . . . . . . . . . . . . . . . 191

# Foreword

## by Dr Mark McKergow

As a solution-focused consultant and facilitator for over 20 years, the one constant in my work has been taking phone calls from leaders and managers along the lines of "I wonder if you can come and work with a team?". The importance of team coaching has never been higher. In the old days, people used to call it 'team building', which seemed to mostly be an opportunity for the team to do something together other than their normal work – going bowling, having a few drinks, or even – if nothing else could be found – getting in a consultant for a 'training day'. While all this would easlily meet the participants' desire for a day out, the benefits to all concerned were not always obvious.

Over the past two decades the idea of team coaching (as opposed to team building) has made great strides. Getting a team together to really focus on what they actually do together – as opposed to having a fun social time – is a valuable opportunity. Making the most of the opportunity is another matter. I personally suffered at the hands of experts who, having been trained in the 1970s, saw their role as 'tearing the team apart and then putting it back together'. Encounter sessions, criticism, psychological bullying in the guide of 'truthful feedback' were all part of the recipe for leaving teams in a mess – which allegedly showed what a mess they had been in already, 'under the surface'.

Fortunately, the new millenium has brought with it many new ideas which support team development in constructive, generative and effective ways. The rise of interest in positive psychology and strengths based work and increasing awareness of agile and other iterative methods have meant a new canvas for facilitators, consultants and managers. What you may not realise is that the Solution-Focused (SF) approach pre-dates all those by a decade or more. SF ideas have come from the therapy room into the management world in a stealthy, even invisible way – the work is minimal, and the focus is on the client (and not on the practitioner). There is also no 'official' model for how to do it (unlike Appreciative Inquiry), and so everyone has to develop their own ways of working with the philosophy and practice developed by Steve de Shazer and Insoo Kim Berg in the 1980s and 1990s.

This book makes a valuable addition to the SF coaching bookshelf. Kirsten Dierolf is an amazingly thorough student of de Shazer and Berg, as well as more recent additions to the SF canon. She has not attempted here to develop her own 'model' of team coaching, such as Daniel Meier's excellent *SolutionCircle*. Rather, she has drawn a wider circle by including this and other models such as Ben Furman and Tapani Ahola's *Reteaming*, to create an overarching guide to SF work with teams. She draws widely from the best of the existing work and adds to it with her own techniques and examples. There are over twenty stories from Kirsten's experience of working with teams contained within these pages, each one of which contains nuggets and ideas which are immediately useful in re-thinking a tough situation or orienting oneself for a potentially challenging session.

Kirsten was instrumental in founding SFCT, the professional body for SF consultants and trainers (www.asfct.org), and is a key member of the editorial team for the SFCT journal *InterAction*. She combines a rigourous sense of SF philosophy with a great deal of practical experience. I can think of no better source to learn about SF team coaching, and to build your journey into helping teams with skill and effectiveness.

Mark McKergow
London, April 2014

# Acknowledgements

A book has many parents – even if there is only one person who writes it and is identified as the author. On the one hand, there are the teams that I have been able to work with and who allowed me to celebrate successes and make mistakes. I learned valuable information from them and from the groups of participants in my team coaching workshops and training sessions. They, too, gave me valuable information through their questions and ideas. On the other hand, this book could not have been written without the support and ideas of my solution-focused colleagues. I would like to thank Daniel Meier, Peter Szabo, Peter Röhrig, Ben Furman, Sue Young, Insa Sparrer, Matthias Varga von Kibéd, Fredrike Bannink, and Mark McKergow who supported me with their ideas and feedback.

Great thanks also goes to Dr. Bremer of Books on Demand and Ms. Keller of Buch&media GmbH for production and distribution of the book and Gaile Campbell for her patience in proofreading.

Many thanks go to my family and the people in my company who dealt with my bad moods during the writing and translating of my research. Thanks to all of you for your patience!

# Introduction

Solution-focused team coaching is a simple, respectful and very effective way to develop teams. In addition to the many other publications about solution-focused consulting, which mainly (and with good reason) focus on the purpose, goals and results of solution-focused consulting, this book will explore the foundation and background of solution-focused team coaching and will provide you with a strong foundation for developing your own team coaching processes. You will find the basics and foundations of solution-focused team coaching in Chapter One.

The second chapter of the book examines the differences between solution-focused team coaching and solution-focused individual coaching. Don't worry – you do not have to know a lot about solution-focused individual coaching to be able to understand this chapter and utilize the hints and tricks that are mentioned. You will learn how to stay multi-partial as a team coach, determine what the team coach focuses on and how he or she can listen most effectively.

The tools of solution-focused team coaching are described in the third chapter. Here you can find many exercises and tools for facilitation and the different phases of the team coaching process. There is also a description of other formats you can use for workshops about team coaching. You will learn how to turn team exercises from other fields into solution-focused exercises.

An overview of different team coaching processes is provided in Chapter Four. You will find a description of the team coaching process which we often use at SolutionsAcademy, plus an overview of other useful processes: Daniel Meier's *SolutionCircle* and Ben Furman's and Tapani Ahola's *Reteaming and Twin Star*.

In the fifth chapter, we talk about difficult situations which can arise in team coaching – and not only in team coaching but also in any kind of group facilitation: negative participants, verbal attacks on the coach, nonstop talkers or groups who don't say anything. Maybe this is not very solution-focused, but we have learned from our participants in workshops on team coaching that it is useful to consider the possibility of these situations in advance in order to be prepared should they arise.

In Chapter Six you will find a description of some standard situations in which customers request team coaching: How can I be helpful as a team coach when the request is about solving a conflict, when there are accusations of bullying, if the customer would like to have support in teambuilding, or when I have to coach a "virtual team"?

Apart from theoretical deliberations and practical hints and tips for implementation, this book offers you many case studies that depict situations that have happened to us the way we describe it or in a similar way. We have tried to anonymize the case studies in such a way that no client will be able to recognize themselves. This book also offers learning exercises. You are invited to experiment with the exercises to facilitate your learning, if you so desire. We are always happy to receive feedback and questions.

Kirsten Dierolf
kirsten@kirsten-dierolf.de

# Foundations of Solution-Focused Team Coaching

## Solution-focused team coaching approaches

Solution-focused team coaching rests on the same foundations as solution-focused interviewing, developed by Insoo Kim Berg and Steve de Shazer and many others between 1980 and 2007. Insoo Kim Berg and Steve de Shazer worked primarily in psychotherapy; the only "teams" they encountered in the beginning were families or couples. Even though there is quite a difference between families and teams, it is still possible to learn a lot about helping more than one person by watching the family therapy sessions led by Insoo Kim Berg and Steve de Shazer (for example, the video "Together in the Middle of the Bed" (Shazer & Berg, 1997). In the last two years before her death, Insoo Kim Berg also gave workshops on team coaching. However, to our knowledge she did not write anything about the topic. After Steve de Shazer and Insoo Kim Berg and others had initiated the solution-focused approach in therapy, Mark McKergow and Paul Z Jackson (Jackson & McKergow, 2002), Ben Furman and Tapani Ahola (Furman & Ahola, 2004), Daniel Meier (Meier, 2005), Louis Cauffman and Kirsten Dierolf (Cauffman & Dierolf, 2007), Fredrike Bannink (Bannink, 2010) and many others further developed the ideas of solution-focused therapy and made them accessible to organizations by adapting the language and processes within the organizational context.

In the following material, we apply the foundations of solution-focused work as they have been described by Steve de Shazer, Yvonne Dolan, Harry Korman, and others in their book "More than Miracles" (Shazer, Dolan & Korman, 2007) to organizational team coaching. We will also differentiate the assumptions and philosophical foundations of solution-focused team coaching from other team coaching processes. This differentiation aims at creating clarity for the reader and is definitely not intended to evaluate or deprecate other approaches. We assume that many different consulting approaches work. It would not be very solution-focused to recommend people who have been doing something success-fully with positive feedback from their clients for years to suddenly start doing something different. For clients and people who would like to learn the approach, there are many advantages to clarity: you know what you are learning or buying and what you are not. This is our motivation for differentiating the solution-focused approach from other approaches in other solution-focused literature.

## If it isn't broken, don't fix it

*Solution-focused team coaching revolves around the goals of the team members. The coaching ends when these goals have been met to the satisfaction of all team members.*

If you relate this tenet to team coaching or team development, it sounds simplistic at first. No consultant in their right mind would argue with it at first sight. In solution-focused therapy, the goal of the client is the main focus: as soon as the client has found that the situation is sufficiently better for him or her, therapy ends. The therapist does not enter any of his or her own goals for the client (for example "the holistic development of the client" or "maturity") into the process. This is the same approach used in solution-focused team coaching: it revolves around the goals of the team members and the coaching ends when these have been met to the satisfaction of all team members. The team members decide on the relevant topics, not the consultant.

There are approaches of team coaching whose goal is to achieve a predetermined ideal state of the team. Team role models (e.g. Belbin, 1981) assume that a team works best if there is a good balance of preferred roles taken up by each team member. Personality profiles like MBTI (Briggs Myers & McCaulley, 1992), DISC (Gay, 1999), and Insights

*If there is a solution focused assumption about teams and working organizations, then it is that nobody comes to work in the morning to do a bad job*

(http://www.insights-group.de) propose that the mix of personalities in the team should be a good fit to the main task of the team. It is assumed to be helpful if the team members know about the advantages of other personality types than the one they belong to. Phase models of team development (e.g. Tuckman, 1965) postulate the existence of a typical development of a team and recommend that the leader of the team and the team members react differently depending on the phase the team is currently in. For example, if the team is in the so-called "storming phase," it is recommended that people sit down and agree on standard processes and rules of engagement. Diagnostic instruments and phase models are not used in solution-focused consulting. If the customer wants to engage in a team coaching process after using such an "instrument," the solution- focused team coach would acknowledge the results and try to find out exactly, in concrete terms, the results that the team wants to achieve. This way you end up working with the goals of the team members, rather than working on a postulated ideal that is presumed valid for any team in any situation.

If there is a solution-focused assumption about teams and working organizations, it is that nobody comes to work in the morning to do a bad job. Put in positive terms, this means that each team member wants to contribute to the success of the team. This assumption makes working with teams a lot easier – but we know that this assumption is not always "correct".

## If it works, do more of it

This tenet of solution-focused work points out that there are behaviors, processes, and solutions that encourage every team to work well. The team coach's question for the team: "So what would you like to keep doing the way you're doing it now?" is therefore very important. In a solution-focused team coaching session, the ability of team members to analyze what needs to stay the same is as important as ex-

*In every team there are behaviors, processes, and solutions that already work well.*

19

ploring what needs to be better or different. Many traditional processes for team development focus on questions about predetermined parameters (e.g. team questionnaires about "clarity of the goal," "quality of the environment," "organizational structure," "information management," "commitment," "employee development opportunities," and "internal and external communication"). Team members fill in such a questionnaire and discuss the evaluation with the team coach. In traditional team development, most team coaches will focus on the weaknesses shown in the evaluation. If, for example, the result is that many team members think that "communication" is "not satisfactory," the team coach might recommend a communication workshop and assume that he or she knows what good communication is in general and what it means for this team. A solution-focused team coach would not make that assumption, but would try to find out what is already working well in the existing communication and what improved communication would look like in detail.

In the solution-focused approach, we look closely at how team members manage sustain the processes and behaviors that are working well. For example, if someone in the team states something like: "There is a good team atmosphere here, even though things are difficult," the team coach will ask: "Your comment is interesting – can you tell me how you managed to keep up a good team atmosphere? What are you doing to create and maintain this good team atmosphere? What is each team member doing individually? What are you doing as a group? What does the team leader contribute?"

## If it's not working, do something different

This solution-focused tenet is aimed at the consultant as well as the team. While this principle is as simple and obvious as the previous one, it is often not put into practice. For example, the team has a good idea for the simplification of a process designed to save money. The simplification is applied. In the application, however, numerous difficulties crop up. The plan simply doesn't want to work. Instead of going back to what worked before and rethinking the process, many teams will try to implement the new process with fierce determination. The failure is attributed to the team members and not to the fact that something is simply not working. Instead of trying more intensively to do what is not working, it would be easier and more effective to try something different.

Example 1: **Automatic travel expenses**

A company automated their travel expense compensation form in order to free up time in the bookkeeping department. Instead of putting all the travel expense receipts in an envelope and sending it to the bookkeeping department via internal mail, along with a home grown Excel sheet, the sales staff was asked to fill in a standard SAP-form which would be automatically processed by the system. In order to be able to identify the individual salesperson, the system asked for their employee number, the department number, a number for the type of travel. etc. A small team of German and a slightly larger team of Polish employees were there to help and ensure that travel expenses were reimbursed correctly. In theory, this was a good idea.

To everybody's surprise, however, it proved to be quite difficult for the sales staff to fill in the form correctly. Chaos ensued. In the team coaching session with the bookkeeping team, the team members talked a lot about all the attempts they had undertaken to help the salespeople with the SAP form. Unfavorable assumptions were shared, such as ("they are simply too...") and people started blaming each other: "Of course, when they call you, you quickly fill in the form for them – I don't have that kind of time," etc. Training the sales staff also had not worked. Threatening them with negative consequences ("If you keep doing that, we will put your form on the bottom of the stack and you will get your money next year.") hadn't either. Nevertheless, the bookkeeping team wanted to intensify their attempts: "We just have to FORCE them to come to our trainings!"

> We assume that every team wants to cooperate.

21

*I asked first how they were coping with the situation: "Cynicism!" "Oh, well, some of the sales people are actually quite nice" or "Well, the form isn't that easy and we understand..."*

*Then we thought about what – if anything – was still working a little bit. The participants mentioned that when they were talking individually with the salespeople things worked pretty well. However, they no longer wanted to do this because it cost them too much time. "If you sit in the same room and are able to explain exactly where they have to put which number, even the laziest salesperson will understand what to do." After a few more minutes of brainstorming one participant had an idea: The team could start holding weekly office hours. People could drop in, and the team could also invite individual salespeople who consistently had difficulties filling in the form, to come in during these office hours in order to have their questions answered. A few months later I asked how this concept had proven to be successful and learned that it had been. Therefore, if something doesn't work, do something different.*

It is also wise for the consultant to do something different if something they are doing isn't working. We assume that every team wants to cooperate and that any team behavior shows cooperation (even though it might not look like that initially.) When the team lets us know that whatever is happening at the moment is not working, we should be grateful and ask what might be useful instead. This way, we refrain from assuming that the team is currently "in denial," "resistant" or "in the storming phase," and we only have to intensify our endeavors. In our experience this attitude makes the life of the team coach much easier. We can then steer the process without needing to know more about team than what is currently useful within the team itself. Our job is to help the team identify their goal and move toward it and to strengthen the positive signals of cooperation. Steve de

*Steve de Shazer once said that you simply have to keep your rapport with your clients – you don't have to do anything specifically to create it or to work on it.*

Shazer once said that you simply have to keep your rapport with your clients – you don't have to do anything specifically to create it or to work on it.

Example 2: **The problem on the table**

*A Swedish corporation had bought Italian and German medium-sized companies. The Italian as well as the German company were working in the area of automotive parts. To facilitate the integration of the two companies, the Swedish corporation wanted to develop a joint European sales strategy. Much to their dismay, this seemed much more difficult to execute than expected. On the one hand, the teams were not communicating often enough with one another. On the other hand, the incentives for the sales force were structured in such a way that working together actually was discouraged rather than incentivized. Cultural differences didn't make it easier. We had spent the first workshop trying to create an understanding of the differences and similarities between cultures, and the team had developed a detailed action plan. They had agreed to implement the action plan before the next meeting.*

*In the next meeting it turned out that almost nothing had happened, although both teams had been very confident. There had been a confidence scale between 1 and 10 (10 was very confident that the agreed measures were useful and could be implemented) and the team members had stated their confidence at an 8-9. When nothing had happened in the meantime, my first impulse as a team coach was to feel responsible: "What had I done wrong?" Luckily I remembered the solution-focused reaction to experiments in individual coaching. If the clients don't do the experiment, we don't see this as a lack of cooperation with the coach – to the contrary, we see it as cooperation with the process. The clients do what makes sense to them and is useful for them, even though it is something different than was agreed.*

*Instead of "holding the team accountable" and talking in detail about why what they had said they would do wasn't done, thereby endan-*

gering the cooperation between me and the team, I asked what they would need to see happening today so this time we could actually make progress in the desired direction. The leader of the German team got very angry and shouted: "We have to put the problems on the table – we can't go on like that. We want to collaborate, but the way we are working at the moment is getting us nowhere." Many team members were nodding in agreement. I quickly asked what would be better if the problems were on the table; I received answers such as they would have better clarity and would know exactly what they needed to work on. As a solution-focused consultant, I really didn't like the idea of this process, but it was the process the participants preferred and thought useful. So I agreed that we would put the problems on the table and sent the participants into a coffee break (this is good advice for all team coaches – if you don't know how to go on, call a coffee break to have time to think.) I used the coffee break to call my colleague Daniel Meier and was lucky enough that he picked up the phone. He told me the story of a team coaching situation that had actually "put the problems on the table." He had asked all participants to write the most important problems on index cards and literally put them on the table.

My workshop took place in a wonderful Italian conference hotel. In the middle of the room we had a large antique table which I used for this exercise after the coffee break. The participants wrote the perceived problems on index cards (5 per participant – there is a limit to how many problems are useful) and put them on the table. We then clustered the most important problems. I then worked with the group to turn the three most important problems into goals (e.g. problem: "our incentive structure doesn't fit to our goals" into "what do we have to do to create an incentive structure that works.") The participants then formed small groups to work on these goals.

Especially in problem-oriented environments, participants sometimes are very skeptical about the solution-focused process – they don't think *it is possible to create an improvement without a thorough analysis of the problem. Solution-focused consultants should see this attitude as an attempt to cooperate with us and to show commitment toward a good result. Of course, we shouldn't completely let go of our responsibility for the process and enter into a detailed analysis of the problem (because it most often leads to an analysis of who is to blame), but we should take issues and problems seriously. Daily business often lacks situations in which employees can talk openly about what's not working. It is just like individual coaching; we shouldn't simply ignore the suffering of the participant(s). What is most important is that every behavior of the team should be viewed as a form of cooperation (even when it doesn't look that way) and if what we are currently doing is not working then we should talk to the participants and do something different.*

## Small steps can lead to big changes

Just like in an individual coaching situation, we also assume in team coaching that the solution or improvement happens in small steps between sessions and not always due to a surprising "AHA-moment" in the session. Solution-

*Every little step can change everything in our clients' lives and new interactions can always become possible*

focused conversations are usually very effective, but not particularly spectacular. That's why they are not very suitable for reality television shows. We assume that every little step can change everything in our clients' lives and new interactions can always become possible. Due to the complexity of human interactions, it is hard to plan which action will result in which change. It is best to stay in the experimentation mode: if something works, do more of it; if something doesn't work, do something different. We therefore prefer shorter processes with a good contract negotiation, clarification of what needs to happen, and a good follow-up of the team's goals.

A typical team coaching process looks like this:

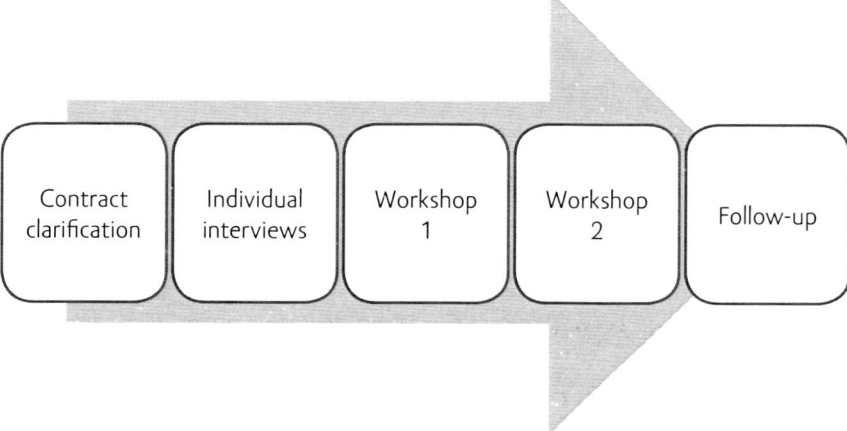

The contract clarification is most often the conversation with the human resource department and the team leader. The individual interviews are short conversations with as many team members as possible. After the interviews, the team receives a report on the interviews and on the topics that were mentioned as important for the workshop. Most often the workshops are rather short, 4-6 hours. The first workshop is usually a little longer than the second. The follow-up is either a face-to-face meeting, or a teleconference 4-6 months after the start of the process, or it is preceded by telephone interviews with team members about what worked well and what still needs attention.

*We shouldn't simply ignore the suffering of the participants.*

This kind of process fits well with today's organizational context: on the one hand, you don't need a lot of time from the team members and they are not away from their desks for a long time, and on the other hand, the transfer of the results of the team coaching into the daily operations of the team is almost inevitable. It is obvious that there is a good chance for a "return on investment." Naturally, if the team members do not want to improve anything or do not have to improve anything, this is different. But since you noticed this early in the team interviews, you can save time and effort by simply not engaging in the rest of the process. In such a situation it makes sense to talk to the human resource department or the team leadership and enable them to create the conditions in which the team members want to change something. Many companies are familiar with incremental processes through methods like "continuous improvement process" or "total quality management." The solution-focused tool, "scaling," is very useful for making signs of progress visible. You can find more information on scaling in the chapter on tools.

Sometimes very ambitious teams have a difficult time understanding that in solution-focused team coaching, we don't start out by planning the whole process of goal achievement. We don't set detailed milestones, assign people who are responsible, or allocate a budget

*Solution-focused processes work with experimentation and, observation of results, far away from the usual planning frenzy and "feasibilitis."*

and an integrated project plan right from the beginning. Our processes work with experimentation, observation of first successes far away from the usual planning frenzy which Daniel Meier and Peter Szabo rightfully call "feasibilitis". Most often team coaching is called for when there is a need to clarify or improve human interactions, to develop a strategy, to improve collaboration, or to deal with conflicts. In these areas you cannot really predict what will happen after each step. This is why it makes little sense to plan further than the next visible steps. The idea behind wanting to plan everything in detail is most often the desire to ensure success. When we explain that success is more likely and that the process will be a better fit if the topic stays on the agenda (and people continue to talk about what has already been achieved and what still has to happen), most teams understand that this kind of process will create a successful result. In software development, this kind of incremental process has already been established as a working method. It is called "Scrum" or "Agile Project Management." These are processes that can be referenced to explain the rationale behind solution-focused team coaching.

# The solution is not necessarily directly related to the problem

Many requests for team development or team coaching start with a description of the problem – either by the human resource department or by the team leaders. In contrast to many other approaches in team coaching, solution-focused team coaching does not start by raising the awareness of the problem and then move on via problem analysis to a solution of the problem. It rather tries to convert problems into goals. The problems that are mentioned are acknowledged and turned into goals by asking solution-focused questions (e. g. "What instead" or "Suppose the problem was solved, what would be better? – how would you notice?") Tapani Ahola and Ben Furman write in their book "Twin Star" (Furman & Ahola, 2004)

*We convert problems into goals – that is why a detailed analysis of the problem is not necessary.*

*The analysis of problems often leads to a vicious cycle!*

> "For every problem there is a corresponding goal; we just have to find it and then turn the problem into that corresponding goal. For example, if the problem is that there is no communication in the company, the corresponding goal for that problem is for there to be communication."

There are two reasons for doing without the analysis of problems: on the one hand, it is not possible to determine the root cause in a complex world with free interdependent decision-makers; on the other hand, problem analyses often lead to vicious cycles within companies. Ben Furman and Tapani Ahola describe this cycle in "Twin Star" (2004) as: focusing on problems ▶ analysing their causes ▶ accusatory explanations ▶ need to defend ▶ bad frame of mind ▶ no creative solutions ▶ no improvement ▶ explaining the lack of involvement ▶ new accusatory explanations, etc. We have often encountered such spirals in contract negotiations.

*Example 3:* **The dominant boss – the disempowered team leader**

*I was called by a competent and friendly HR-professional in training and development about whether I had time for a difficult team coaching. The situation seemed to be stalled, the works council had been contacted ... and would I be willing to try to help – she was at the end of her rope. If I wasn't able to resolve the situation, at least we would have made the effort. I was a bit surprised by her description of the situation. The HR-professional had always been positive and optimistic when I had taken on jobs for her before. Of course, I was interested in finding out more. I asked to talk to the team leader, the two team leaders who reported to her and several team members.*

*In my conversation with the team leader, I discovered that one of the group leaders was new to the team and wasn't accepted by the others. He was seen as incompetent and presumptuous. The team members confirmed this, although I did not ask for that information; instead, I asked how they would notice that the team is working well and that everyone is looking forward to coming to work in the morning willing to do their best.*

*The new group leader had a completely different perspective: his dominant boss was secretly conspiring with the other team members and wanted to bully him out of his position. In his view this was very obvious; his boss was constantly criticizing him in front of his team and also in front of senior managers. It was impossible to re-establish any authority in front of the team after such incidents. This was also why he had involved the works council.*

*I then contacted the representative of the works council who was a very wise and mature man. He advised to "keep this as low profile as possible" and to refrain from legal or formal action in this case.*

*The team had entered the negative spiral described by Ben and Tapani. For the group leader, the problem was clear:*

1) Focusing on problems: his boss does not want him in this position.

2) Analyzing their causes: this is why she is undermining him.

3) Accusatory explanations: she is not able to tolerate a man in a position of authority. She is too dominant herself and is not able to delegate decisions or competencies.

4) Need to defend: now he has to make sure to defend his authority.

5) Bad frame of mind: he starts to use an inadequate and unfriendly tone in his conversations with his group members.

6) No creative solutions: he sees that there are problems in his group, but he thinks that they are caused by his boss' behavior.

7) No improvement: his boss continues to criticize him – he acts just like before.

8) Explaining the lack of involvement: he assumes that she never wanted him on the team in the first place and contacts the works council.

Exercise 1:  **Practicing escalation**

Why don't you try a little exercise: Use the above steps and jot down the vicious cycle for the team and boss – you will see how easy this is!

Naturally, this vicious cycle is only one of many possible explanations, and as such it is not really necessary for solution-focused practice. In the ensuing team process, it was very important to define the goal for the team together with the team leader and the boss. It was also crucial to get the negative assumptions and accusations of both parties out of the way. If the leadership is not thinking and pulling in one direction, it is difficult for the team. In a half-day workshop, I was able to clarify goals for their future collaboration and how reaching those goals would make a difference in the future. We spent a long time working on a detailed picture of a best case scenario in six months. We also worked on what made both confident that they could achieve this. Both the boss and the team leader were able to state what needs to be different without attacking the other.

After two months the team had realized a positive change. We proceeded with a team coaching day with the team leader and his team. Since the team had already noticed improvements, they were able to give appreciative feedback. They were also able to state which changes they would like from their team leader and each other. The team leader was able to accept the feedback (probably because of the positive experiences of the two previous months) and was able to plan concrete steps for further improvement of the atmosphere.

*Solution-focused team coaching (as well as solution-focused individual coaching or therapy) is mainly about the present and the future that is created together.*

Working on the goal proved to be simple and clear. Had we entered into an analysis of the problem, most probably there would have been further focus on the deficits of each involved person.

Solution-focused team coaching (as well as solution-focused individual coaching or therapy) is mainly about the present and the future that is created together. It is about making progress possible by looking for resources and clues which give confidence that the desired state can be reached.

At the SOL world conference in Cologne in 2008, Mark McKergow presented an interesting model of different consulting approaches:

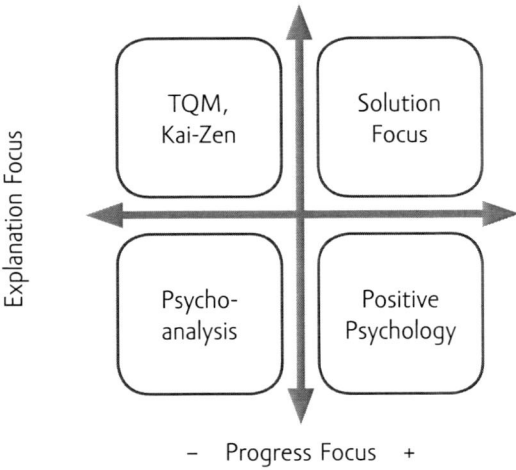

This graph simplifies reality; obviously there are many resource-oriented psychoanalysts and there are also progress-oriented representatives of positive psychology. However, the graph shows what solution-focused team coaching is about: achieving progress and identifying the relevant resources for that progress and not focusing on the negative situation or identifying faults.

## The language for solution development is different from that needed to describe a problem

A lot has already been said about this point in this book. What still needs to be mentioned is that when the team, the team leader or the consultant describe a problem and look for its causes, the problem often seems more difficult and more stable than is actually the case.

Some problems are relatively simple and can be viewed in a narrowly defined framework or system: a bicyclist notices that her bicycle is hobbling along rather than running smoothly. The brake isn't working either. She looks down and realizes that she has a flat tire. The solution seems directly connected to the problem: the tire is repaired and our bicyclist can continue riding safely and comfortably.

When people in teams look for root causes to complex topics (like the collaboration of people), they often don't mention directly observable causes (for example, "the team is not as productive as it could be because it hasn't yet mastered the new software. Training would be useful.") The causes that are mentioned are usually related to a psychological, philosophical or other system of thought (for example, "the team is not as productive as it could be because they haven't taken on board the change to the new product. They're still in the resistance phase. We should work on the ability of the team to deal with changes.")

*We listen to what the team wants, which resources and exceptions are already there and start moving.*

In therapy, diagnoses are often mistaken for causes: the patient "has" a depression (de Shazer, 1997, p. 135). This leads to the perception that the patient's sadness and lack of motivation are a consequence of deeper psychological processes. Instead of working on what should get better and accompanying the patient by taking small steps toward the joy of life and activity (or whatever the patient wants), a lot of time is spent with the exploration of the causes of the depression (childhood, trauma etc.) Of course, this may work, but it usually takes a much longer time than solution-focused therapy (Berg, 2008). In team coaching, there may be various diagnostic systems which lend greater stability to the problem than is necessary. These systems can be derived from psychology (personality profiles, analysis of the leadership position, etc.) or from management science (change models, benchmarking, generic strategic success models). In solution-focused team coaching, however, we completely eliminate these systems. We listen to what the team wants, which resources and exceptions are already there, and start moving.

## No problem happens all the time; there are always exceptions that can be utilized

In team coaching, just like in individual coaching, we look for "highlights" and "best practice cases" – which are simply exceptions from the problem. If the team coaching isn't triggered by a problem but by a desire to improve something, we look for instances in which the situation was already similar to the way the team wants it to be. This is especially important when there is a conflict, but is also especially difficult. After all, who wants to be reminded that "the enemy" was once a friendly and competent person? While these conversations are not easy for the consultant, they are very useful.

Especially in team situations, it can be very useful to ask everybody about a time when something was better than it currently is. By collecting the perceptions of "when it was better," you create two useful conversations: (1) By describing what "better" is, everybody becomes clear on what exactly they are looking for, and (2) By recognizing that something like this has already happened in some ways, the team becomes more confident that the desired state can be reached.

*Example 4:* **The team scale**

A team wanted their boss to defend them against the ever-increasing number of projects which the organization required them to participate in. They wanted him to clarify priorities within the organization. They felt like they never had the possibility to finish anything the way they would like to. It was very important for the team to be able to contribute something meaningful to the organization, but their motivation was suffering under the high-pressure of things that they could never do as well as they wanted. The boss had listened to the discussion and had just started a motivational speech in the direction of "but we have to be open to change – resistance is negative..." and was then stopped in his tracks by the team.

Before anybody could escalate the situation, I asked the boss whether he wanted to listen to the good reasons of his team first. I assured him that after he listened to his team, he would have the opportunity to state his good reasons. The ensuing discussion was very open and appreciative of everybody's perceptions. The team created a list of all projects and the boss was a little shocked. He said that the reputation of the team in the organization was very important and that he was trying to make the team look good. Constantly rejecting projects wouldn't create a good reputation. A new joint goal was born: "Looking good and still only accepting projects that can be completed to the satisfaction of the team and the organization." I asked the team for a scale of 1 to 10. 10 means that this goal has been reached; 1 the opposite. At this point nobody was higher than a 3 (including the boss). When asked when it had already been a little bit better, the team mentioned an interesting exception: a while ago there had been a team role of "change-coordinator." The team member who had fulfilled this function had left the company. I asked what exactly had been helpful when this role was filled (because it is mainly about the useful interactions which this team member made possible). She had

*As solution-focused team coaches, we look for goals that all team members can subscribe to. We facilitate in such a way that everybody's contribution is appreciated.*

*created a list of projects with respective prioritization, the man days, the project status, etc. and was always able to pass on information about team capacity. The team decided to work on a similar concept. The team leader managed to hire a professional project manager and installed a "change board" with three team members who had an overview of all projects and were responsible for informing the team of their respective progress. When we met again after a year, the topic was at an 8 on the scale, and that was good enough for everybody.*

It is naturally not always this easy to find an exception. Sometimes one team member's "highlight" is the "lowlight" of another. As solution-focused team coaches, we look for goals that all team members can subscribe to. We facilitate in such a way that everybody's contribution is appreciated. Everybody has and keeps their right to his or her own perception. Usually looking for exceptions creates a good atmosphere. The team feels that there is progress and that they are now working on concrete solutions.

## The future is both created and negotiable

"Somebody should in his role as this-and-this, he really should have," or "if this-and-this, it's entirely clear that" – who doesn't know these statements from team meetings? And if we are honest, we must admit that we probably have made similar statements ourselves. We keep thinking that we can predict the future. Only in moments of modesty and self-awareness do we realize that this is not the case. Many consulting approaches sell the safety of "if-then" cycles, e.g. "only if you determine the key performance indicators for your team can you really know whether you're being successful." "Only teams with different personalities can lead to success in this case." In our view, these approaches simplify the complexity of life by generalization and by comparison of incomparable situations.

Seeing the future as both created and negotiable creates hope – if there are no predetermined "if-then" connections, situations can improve which before had seemed hopeless. I have often seen teams find their way back to a fruitful collaboration who previously hadn't thought it possible.

Example 5: **The initiative for excellence that backfired**

*A banking team had suffered through an "initiative for excellence" that was led by an internal group of consultants. The consultants had observed the banking team at all international locations. Without communicating much with the team, they found the team's performance was lower than that of similar teams at other banks. Something needed to be done. The team met with the consultants to devise a strategy. The consultants provided feedback to the team that they were not really doing good work. To improve they would use the remaining time of the same meeting to develop a vision for the team, a mission statement, and team values. You can imagine how engaged the team members were in this process. Nobody took this exercise seriously because they hadn't been taken seriously. Nothing improved and, in fact, the pressure rose and rose. After six months, the team and the consultants had reached a low point of accusing each other. There was another meeting but nobody said anything. The boss of the internal consulting team tried to get somebody to talk: "You must say something; something is wrong here!" She received the following answer: "No, no, everything's okay. Let's just continue with your program." The internal consultant started a debate: "Well, your body language is saying something different – I can interpret body language, I was trained in this!" Again, the meeting ended in a catastrophe of everybody accusing everybody else. I was called in by the internal consultant to help the team communicate more openly. She didn't see any need to change her own behavior. The team, in her view, wasn't open to change and it was necessary to "unfreeze" them. Looking at this situation you would normally think that the situation was not salvageable – however, if you think that the future can be both negotiable and created together, you can at least give it a try. I called all the involved people and asked about the confidence of the team and whether anything could be changed at all.*

*Most team members weren't very confident. They were around a 2-3 on the scale. The confidence that was there resulted from the fact that the problem had now been acknowledged and that I was there as a consultant. When I asked what could increase their confidence, a'most everybody answered that they would need to have a meeting without the internal consultants. I asked the internal consultants whether that would be okay. They were quite desperate, and so they were willing to try anything to turn the situation around. We had a meeting and worked on the goal: "to achieve performance improvements that are necessary to keep the internal consultants away and achieved some concrete measures and process improvement steps. These improvements led to an observable increase in the self-confidence of the team rather quickly. In the next meeting they were able to discuss important issues and find steps toward a solution. Interestingly enough, one of the main topics that was important to all team members was "going back to a situation in which everybody can openly state what they think." When asked how they would notice that the situation was safe enough to openly state what they think, many said they would like to talk about how to criticize each other without hurting each other's feelings. Not everything was going right all the time, so criticism was necessary. However, they definitely did not want to go back to accusations and a defensive stance. Every team member wrote a flipchart with instructions about how they would like to listen to criticism. We put the flipcharts on the wall and everybody walked around and read the requests of their colleagues. Nobody asked for anything that the others weren't willing to do. In the last meeting 12 months after the first contact, all problems had been solved and the team atmosphere and relationships were trusting and open. The performance of the team had increased to the satisfaction of all involved.*

> *Sometimes the only solution is that people stop working together.*

The confidence scale is very useful in seemingly hopeless situations when you want to achieve even a small improvement. Small improvements can lead to bigger improvements and situations become changeable which seemed stuck before. Naturally, this doesn't work all the time. Sometimes the only solution is that people stop working together. When this happens, the situation is clear at least and new beginnings become possible.

# Differences to individual coaching

## Introduction

There are a few differences between solution-focused individual coaching and solution-focused team coaching. When you are dealing with several people, each of these people is likely to have a different goal for the team coaching. It is therefore more difficult to come to a good definition of the goal with the team than it is with an individual. You can also have a situation in which team members have conflicting goals. The solution-focused approach offers several possibilities to set goals with groups in such a way that everybody is happy with the process and the resulting goals. You can find more about these possibilities in our chapter on "Tools" under "Goal Setting".

Another important difference is that facilitating the conversation is more difficult when you have several people involved. Every participant of team coaching wants to be appreciated. It is important to facilitate each contribution in such a way that every team member feels heard. In order to achieve this, the team coach not only needs to have coaching skills, but needs facilitation skills, as well. In order to facilitate well (and also in order to coach well), the team coach needs the acceptance and trust of the team. As mentioned above, Steve de Shazer took rapport as something that you simply have to take care of not losing. Generating trust and acceptance is not something in which you should put in a lot of extra effort. In my experience, it actually becomes more difficult if you do many things to generate rapport which you would usually not do in a normal encounter with a group of people. The whole situation quickly becomes unnatural and awkward, which can lead to a bad start in team coaching. In many other approaches you can find recommendations on how to generate rapport. The coach is asked to "pace" movements and body postures of individual team members by imitating them. Once he or she has done this long enough, he or she can start "leading" the group and get the team members to follow his or her movements and body language. The idea is based on the fact that you can observe similarities in the movement patterns between two people in a successful therapeutic conversation (for example, the research of F. Ramseyer and W. Tschacher, 2008, pp. 329-348), but it is a little bit of a chicken and egg situation: are the patterns of movement similar because people understand each other well, or does a good understanding lead to people's patterns of movement becoming similar? Using Occam's razor and following the old adage: "The simplest explanation is always the best," solution-focused consultants assume a good relationship and try not to lose it.

So maybe it makes sense to think about the opposite. What does somebody have to do to guarantee the destruction of a good working relationship between the consultant and his or her clients? Here are some recommendations (which we hope you won't take seriously): most importantly the consultant should avoid listening to his or her clients. The consultant should insist on his or her own interpretations and take any reply from the clients as a sign of resistance. The agenda of the team coaching should primarily consist of points important to the consultant. There should never be room for any agenda items that the team wants to deal with. A good idea for the destruction of the working relationship is also taking the side of one of two groups. It is especially nice to consistently agree with the boss and fight on the side of the boss against the team. It is probably also useful for the destruction of a good working relationship when the consultant uses a completely different language than the team. If the team consists of elegant bankers, the consultant should take care to use soft pedagogical language. Distinguishing yourself by a completely different outward appearance than the one of your clients can also prevent a good working relationship, e.g. if the team spends their day in suit and tie, the consultant could wear a miniskirt or torn jeans and a T-shirt. If the team is used to elegant PowerPoint presentations, the consultant should insist on using badly written flipcharts in his or her facilitation.

*Each team member has their own goals.*

When the solution-focused consultant adheres to Steve de Shazer's advice and simply takes care not to disturb the good working relationship, it is helpful to turn the above advice around. We don't think that you can produce a list of things that a consultant needs to do in order not to endanger a good working relationship. There are consultants who always wear jeans and T-shirts and work effectively with wide-ranging clients. There are other consultants who wear suit and tie even when they are working in the public sector. When you look at Steve de Shazer, you may not see someone who conveys the image of timeless elegance or therapeutic authority. What disturbs the respective working relationship is always decided in the interaction between consultant and client. It is very difficult to give general advice. In solution-focused consulting, we try to speak the language of our clients. Experience shows that this tends to lead to a good collaboration between consultant and clients; therefore, the only advice that we give is to listen really well to the words of our clients. If you concentrate too hard on many other things that you have to get right in order not to endanger the relationship, you will have less time and attention to spend on the important things: listening and exploring the client's goals, resources and exceptions and first steps.

When you are working with teams, there is also the question who belongs to the team, who needs to be asked, who needs to participate in which event. In solution-focused family therapy you work with everybody who is interested in coming and working on a solution. It is important that everybody feels welcome and invited. This is also a good strategy for team coaching. In an organizational context it makes sense to understand who belongs to the team, who has which competence to decide what, who has a stake in the solution, etc. In organizations there are more formal rules for that than in families, and in our experience you can avoid misunderstandings if you know beforehand who decides what and what the relevant framework for decisions is.

One advantage in working with teams is that you have many involved people in the room with you. In individual coaching you would have to ask, "What do you think your boss would say?" In the team coaching situation the boss is probably in the room, and you can ask directly. Many conversations which happen after the coaching sessions in individual coaching can happen immediately and are facilitated by the team coach.

## Multipartiality

In the team coaching process, there are usually several people with differing interests. We deal with this point in a similar fashion as in solution- focused couples or family therapy. These ideas go back to Ivan Boszormenyi-Nagy and Geraldine Spark. They were the first to speak about "multi-directional partiality" in their book "Invisible Loyalties" of 1973. This concept of multi-directional partiality was then taken up by solution-focused therapists.

*The benefit for clients is that the therapist seems to be standing on both sides. He or she isn't "neutral" – but involved and engaged for the benefit of both parties.*

Phillip Ziegler and Tobey Hiller explore this helpful standpoint for therapists in their book "Recreating Partnerships" from 2001. It is a standpoint of "active neutrality" or of "multi-partiality" (Ziegler & Hiller, 2001, pp. 39-41) The benefit for clients is that the therapist seems to be standing on both sides. He or she isn't "neutral" – but involved and engaged for the benefit of both parties. I also recommend this attitude for team coaches. The only difficulty here is that you have more than two people on whose sides you should try to be. It is therefore a little bit more difficult yet very rewarding to strive for a "multi-partial" standpoint. The consultant is engaged, is not drawn into the accusations or complaints of any one party, and is collaborating with everyone to find a solution.

Nothing is easier than this, right? Well, but how does it work? How do you maintain a standpoint of multi-partiality? Hiller and Ziegler discuss two very important points:

- The consultant should accept the assumption and demonstrate that reality can always be seen from various perspectives. The meaning isn't fixed, but changeable and differing perspectives can always leads to conflicts.

- The consultant should also try and subscribe to an attitude of curious "not-knowing."

The first point is especially important in team coaching. Participants
notice the attitude of the consultant
when the team coach doesn't try to
level differences. The team coach lis-

*Curious: "Not-Knowing" is also important for the team coach.*

tens to every participant's opinion and contribution and is interested in
it. He or she doesn't try to question anybody's perception. For example, if
an employee claims that he or she is constantly working overtime because
a colleague fails to enter data into the system correctly, the team coach
will accept this perception at face value. If the colleague then contradicts,
his or her perception is taken as equally "true." The team coach will then
try to achieve a constructive conversation that acknowledges both perspectives. After acknowledging the problem, he or she might ask: "Suppose this problem was solved for both of you, how would you notice?" or
"What kind of exceptions have you already noticed?" etc. For the solution-
focused team coach, each participant's perspective is equally "true" in that
moment.

Curious "Not-Knowing" is also important for the team coach. Instead of
engaging in elaborate analyses of which structures and processes brought
forth the current situation or otherwise indulging in our own theories,
solution-focused team coaches try to listen intensively. Of course, solution-
focused team coaches also have their own frame of reference and cannot
"not use their own frame of reference". Our frame of reference, however,
stands back in favour of the exploration of the frame of reference of our
clients. If this proves too difficult, we just pretend to do that.

When you look at it from the pragmatic side there are a few behaviours
which are useful to support the multiparty of the consultant: If there are
interviews before a possible workshop, it is important to be transparent
about who is being called, who isn't being called and why. If at all possible, it is best to be able to talk to everybody beforehand. It is equally important to take care to talk to the team leader, for example, during breaks
in the workshop. During a workshop, it makes sense to have an equal

amount of speaking time for everybody. If somebody conveys confidential information to the team coach, it is important to deal with it sensitively.

Each contribution during the workshop should be accepted with appreciation. In contrast to other coaches, solution-focused team coaches sometimes interrupt. If a participant has a difficult time getting out of the complaining mode, we try to turn the conversation around and ask: "What needs to be different?" Such a process makes it easy to stay curious and acknowledge and validate the perspectives and goals of each team member.

Exercise 2:  **Multipartiality**

Think about how you would notice that somebody is on your side in a controversial conversation or in a meeting. How does this person act and what does it look like exactly? Write "guidelines for being on my side." Then think about which of these behaviors would also be good for multipartial facilitation and experiment with these behaviors in your next team facilitation.

Exercise 3:  **"Together in the middle of the bed"**

The video "Together in the middle of the bed" by Steve de Shazer and Insoo Kim Berg provides a good opportunity to observe multi-partial behavior. It is a first session in couple's therapy with a married couple. The first minutes of this session provide many clues. Steve de Shazer is the therapist. It is very noticeable that he does not evaluate or interpret the statements by the husband or by the wife, but simply lets them stand. He takes care to allocate equal speaking time to each partner. He asks the husband about the possible perspective of his wife and vice versa. When one of them starts enter-

*Other than other coaches solution-focused team coaches sometimes interrupt.*

ing into a longer phase of complaining, he interrupts softly and says, "We'll get back to that." Steve de Shazer works on small, observable signs of improvement. These are all means that you can use in team coaching, especially in conflict situations. Watch the video (you can order it at www.sfbta.org) and maybe you will notice other techniques that you can transfer and use in your team coaching.

## Listening

Listening is another very important tool for solution-focused team coaching. Solution-focused listening is different from "active listening." Active listening is about enabling the consultant to understand the client as exactly as possible. The techniques for achieving this are a consultant's repetition of what the clients say in their own words. The technical term here is "paraphrasing." Solution-focused listening is not

*The solution-focused team coach listens most intensively when the team is talking about what they want, about resources or other things that give the team confidence that improvement is possible.*

about exact understanding. We assume that in each interaction meanings are created and negotiated between the conversation partners and that understanding 100% correctly is neither possible nor necessary. Listening is more about not disturbing the relationship between consultant and team, and that the team has the impression that a consultant understands what they're trying to say and is working on a solution together with them. The solution-focused team coach listens most intensively when the team is talking about what they want, such as resources or other things that give the team confidence that improvement is possible.

Exercise 4:  **Listening**

Watch a debate on television (e.g. in a talk show) and listen in a goal and resource oriented fashion. Take a piece of paper per participant of the discussion. Jot down: "What does this person want?" (stated as the presence of something, not the absence. For example, not: "What does this person want to avoid?" and "Which resources can I perceive in this person – what makes me confident that he or she can reach this goal?")

## Using the language of your clients

Nothing creates the feeling of being understood better than when the consultant is using the language of the team. This can be quite difficult, especially when the team is working in a field that is completely foreign to the consultant. Therefore, we have always found it very valuable to know a little bit about what the team does, which words are being used and which context the team is working in before engaging in team coaching. We are not engaging in a diagnosis or analysis (even though it might look this way from the outside), but we are trying to learn the language of the team to be able to connect.

*We are trying to learn the language of the team to be able to connect.*

When we are talking about language we are not only talking about the vocabulary; we are speaking more generally about the culture, the "grammar" of the team. If everybody shows up every day in jeans we will not wear our pinstriped suit. If it is a team of down-to-earth high school graduates, we will not boast about our university degrees. If we are working for an international consultancy in which intelligence and qualification play a large role, it might happen that we mention our credentials quickly. We believe that just like in individual coaching, the trust and confidence of the team concerning the consultant and their belief that his or her ability will help them move forward is one of the main success factors of coaching.

# Summary

*Solution Focused Tenets*

- If it isn't broken, don't fix it: The only relevant focus is what the client wants
- If it works, do more of it: In every team there are things that are still working
- If it's not working, do something different: This tenet is not only valid for clients, but also for consultants
- Small steps can lead to big changes: no master plan of the process from 0 (or 1) to miracle
- The solution is not necessarily directly related to the problem: no analysis of the problem
- The language for solution development is different from that needed to describe a problem: it's about a solution and not about who's to blame – brainstorming, not blamestorming, as Ben Furman says.
- No problem happens all the time; there are always exceptions that can be utilized: Every team has relevant useful experiences and exceptions
- The future is both created and negotiable: planning concrete first steps instead of large psychological or management surveys and instruments

*Differences to individual coaching*

- Multipartiality
- Listening for goals and resources
- Using the language of your clients

*There is no "normal" team coaching process. No plan survives the crash with reality.*

# Tools

"But how does this work in practice?" you've probably already been asking yourself. In the following discussion, we would like to present a few tools for facilitation of team coaching processes. We will follow the structure of a "normal" team coaching process. It is important to realize, though, that there is actually no "normal" team coaching process. Just as in individual coaching, the team coach needs to react flexibly to the requirements of each situation with the team. Naturally, this is more difficult if you have to agree with more than one person about what would be useful. Nevertheless, it is more useful to do what is important in the moment with the team than what you had planned in your preparation time.

## Good working relationship

As already stated, it is important not to lose the good working relationship with your clients. This is mainly true for the working relationship between consultant and clients. In team coaching, not only the relationship between consultant and client is important, but also the relationships of the team members to each other. It can be very useful to take care in the beginning of the team coaching process that a confident and positive atmosphere can develop. The more hope the team has that something can improve, the more likely the improvement. The following will provide you with a few exercises that can be useful.

### "Glues Clues"

Glues clues is exercise for teams who know each other well and are not in horrible conflict at the moment. It's a bit humorous. What is being glued are Post-It notes. In a group of a maximum of eight participants, ask each participant to write Post-it notes for all the other participants and then stick them to the back of the chairs of the other participants or even to the backs of the participants. When all participants are done writing and gluing, everybody may read the Post-It notes that were written for him or her.

What you ask the participants to write onto the Post-it notes, should reflect the issue at hand:

- a personal strength that I observed in you
- something about you that makes me confident that we can solve the problem together
- something that I appreciate in the way we work together
- something positive that I heard from others about you
- something that you should keep doing

For some people this exercise is initially a bit embarrassing. At least in central Europe we are not so used to making compliments. When you do engage participants in this exercise, you will be rewarded by smiling faces of the participants when they are reading their Post-it notes.

## "One for all and all for one!"

Ask the participants to pair up. Every pair should talk about a few things that have recently been going well. The goal of the conversation is to identify four strengths that both have in common. In the next round two pairs talk to each other and try to identify at least two strengths that the four of them share. Once this is successful, two groups of four people (so overall 8 people) try to identify one strength that everybody has in common. If you have an unequal group size, you can also use differently sized groups (for example 3, 5 or 7 people). You can obviously also use other encouraging questions or questions that generate hope like:

- Find things that make you confident that you can improve something.
- Collect positive remarks that you have heard about yourself from customers.

The success of this exercise depends on the company and its culture – take care that this does not become too embarrassing for anyone.

*A personal superlative*

Every participant thinks about something they think they are best at compared to everybody else in the group, for example "the best singer," "the best tennis player," etc. This exercise is very short, funny, and has led to the foundation of choirs, dance and tennis groups in companies. What is important for the atmosphere is that it is clear that this is not a serious competition, but that anything can be mentioned as a "personal superlative", even if it is silly. We usually start by giving our own example: "I think I am best at folding paper planes."

# Pre-session Change

In team coaching, just like in individual coaching, you can build on the positive developments that happened between the time of setting up the meeting and the first meeting.

You can ask "what's better" in the beginning of each team coaching step – even when you're just starting and negotiating the contract ("since you started to think about engaging in the team coaching process, what has already happened in the right direction?") When you start the team coaching process with individual interviews, you can ask this question at the beginning of each interview. It can be an important point in a report or be the start of any meeting. This question focuses the attention on progress and also clarifies what exactly should be better and what is the right direction. It also creates confidence. It is often easier to start when the first step has been taken.

There are the following ways to facilitate a discussion on this question:

*Collecting participants' comments about "What is better in your view?" on a flipchart*

Collecting participants' answers in the plenary is fast and all participants can listen and understand what is important for everybody else. When you're talking about "what's better" in the plenary, the facilitator can also take care that the perception of all participants is acknowledged as valid.

The things one person takes as better do not have to be the same for everybody else. It makes no sense to discuss the differences in perception at this point. When you are facilitating this discussion, you can also help the group to avoid slipping back into the usual "what we think needs to be better."

## Small group discussions about "What is better?"

You can also create small groups instead of having a plenary discussion. The day could begin with small groups going for a walk and talking about "What is better?" Each small group can take a few Post-It notes to jot down their thoughts. Of course, this exercise can also be conducted on tables or standing up. Experience shows that going for a walk takes the longest, small group discussions with seated participants are little bit longer, and discussions when people are standing up need the least time. A walk should be around 30 minutes, the seated small group discussions 20 minutes, and discussions standing up 15 minutes If there are several small groups writing Post-It notes about "What is better?", the answers are usually more varied than when you are working in a plenary. Another advantage of working with Post-It Notes is that you can see how frequently an answer is given. For example, if several small groups notice that the atmosphere has improved, this perception is strengthened by the frequency. In this situation it makes sense to cluster (sort according to topic) the Post-It notes after the exercise. It can also be useful to have a look at these perceived changes in the right direction with the group and talk about which of them should definitely continue. It is also very important that everybody's perception of positive change is acknowledged and validated. For example, if Mr. Jones contradicts, "But I don't think our atmosphere has improved," it is important that the facilitator clarifies that not all changes have to be noticed by everyone. Every team member has their own perception and perspective, and that is the beauty of teamwork. In such situations the facilitator can also invite the group to continue by observing what works in order to establish his or her own multipartiality and appreciation for everybody's contribution:

> *Every team member has their own perspective – that's the beauty of teamwork.*

"Ah, Mr. Jones, that's very interesting! Why don't you think about what Ms. Smith could have observed that tells her that the atmosphere has improved and maybe also think about how you would notice an improvement in the team atmosphere. Please don't give an answer right now – have a think and observe a little bit."

### Speed-dating: What is better?"

"Speed-dating" is a very nice way of starting a workshop day and fun and active fashion. This form has many names and you can also find it described as "the solution onion" in the book 57 SF activities (Röhrig & Clarke, eds. , 2008, pp. 61-65). You divide the group into two groups with the same number of participants. One group stands in an inner circle facing outward; the other group stands in an outside circle facing inward. This way, two participants are standing opposite each other: one in the inside circle, one in the outside circle. The facilitator asks the group to discuss a predetermined question for a few minutes. These can be banal questions like, "How was your trip?" or more meaningful questions like, "What in the workshop are you interested in today?" or "What has already gone in the right direction since we made the appointment for this meeting?" This way of facilitation activates participants, creates a relaxed mood and is fun. Participants can talk about important and not so important topics. You can also try and visualize the answers to the questions by distributing Post-It Notes – however, this creates a more serious mood. If the visualization is necessary or desired, you can also collect the questions after each round and put the results of the exercise on a flipchart.

### Individual work with Post-It notes: "What is better?"

Of course, you can also ask participants to work on the question of "what's better" individually. Each participant writes their answers on Post-It notes. Working individually is oftentimes very helpful because it gives participants time to really think for themselves. In my personal experience, it is a real treasure when you can tap into the creativity and power of observation of many different people this way. Individual work is not often used in teams or groups. It is a format that people are not used to – this is why it might not be appropriate for every situation, especially in the beginning of the workshop. It depends on the group, how important the topic "what's better?" is, and on the momentary mood of the facilitator.

*Work in small groups or pairs on: "What did we get right in the last months?"*

Asking about highlights in the last months is an alternative to the question "what's better?" You can ask small groups or pairs to discuss the question, "What did we get right in the last months?" or "What were good moments in the previous months?" You can find a good description of how to facilitate this in 57 SF activities (Röhrig & Clarke, eds., 2008) in a contribution by Mark McKergow entitled "Sparkling Moments." Depending on the team culture, you can vary the intensity of the question. In the US you would probably ask, "What are you really proud of?" In Germany or Japan you might ask, "What could have gone worse in the last months?" or "What wasn't too bad?"

> *Working individually is oftentimes very helpful because it gives participants the time to really think for themselves.*

## Goal setting

Most traditional methods of setting goals with teams are also appropriate for solution-focused team coaching. The only thing that you need to take care of is to ask solution focused questions. Instead of asking "What is your goal?" You ask for a rich description of the situation when the goal has been achieved, "Suppose you have reached your goal – how would you start noticing it?" Alternative questions are built around fictitious perceptions of other stakeholders in the future, such as "How do you think your boss would notice?" or "How would your customers notice?" Here is a list of possible useful questions:

- "Suppose this team coaching process is very useful for you, how will you know in three months that it was a very good idea to engage in this team coaching process?"

- "How would your boss, your customers, the boss of your boss, other departments, etc. notice that it was worth your time to enter into this team coaching process?"
- "What exactly will they notice is better?"
- "What else?"
- "What else?"
- "What do we need to do, talk about, or decide today that might make this possible?"

*It is important to generate a rich picture of the desired future which is in the influence of the clients. The goal should be stated positively and describe the presence of the new situation and not the absence of what people no longer want.*

It is important to generate a rich picture of the desired future which is in the influence of the clients. The goal should be stated positively, describe the presence of the new situation and not the absence of what people no longer want.

Exercise 5:  **Goal setting**

Take the following goals (goals from our real work with clients) and determine what's "wrong" with them, why they would not be taken at face value as goals in a solution-focused process. You will find the solution on the next page.

1) The legal department would stop being so overworked and incompetent.

2) We need better communication.

3) We should stop constantly blaming each other.

Solution:

1) This goal is not in the influence of our clients and is stated negatively. It also sounds like a negative value statement. Basically, you do not know what should be there instead of overwork and incompetence. A better way of putting it could be, for example, "Our collaboration with the legal department has improved so that we get answers quickly when we have an important request for information."

2) This goal is in the influence of our clients; however, "improved communication" can mean a lot. Ludwig Wittgenstein and Steve de Shazer would call it a term that is defined by "family resemblances." As consultant you would have to ask how people would notice "improved communication." If you clarify the goal in this way, you usually receive first ideas for a solution: "Every morning when everybody is there, we will have a 10 minutes stand up meeting, and we will tell each other what is on our plate for today and discuss the priorities."

3) In this case the topic is also what should not be there instead of what should happen. Clarifying the goal again gets you closer to the solution: "When we have a problem we will talk about how we can solve it. It's not about who's to blame."

There are several ways of facilitating goal setting conversations with teams. Here are a couple of formats:

## Plenary discussion with flipchart

Using a flipchart to visualize the discussion about goals is a quick way of clarifying what needs to happen so that the process is worthwhile. In the goal setting phase, it is especially important that the team agrees on at least the general direction of the desired development. Therefore, all team members should listen to the goals of

*In a solution-focused goal setting process you rarely have conflicting goals.*

everybody else. When you are working with a flipchart in the plenary, that happens automatically. It is important that the facilitator writes down all of the stated goals. In a solution-focused goal setting process, you rarely have conflicting goals because you are talking about what needs to be better after the team coaching process, and not about how to get to that state. In the rare case that you do have conflicting goals, the facilitator can ask for the goal behind the goal before writing anything down on the flipchart. Examples for eliciting the goal behind the goal might be:

- "When you have achieved this, what will be better?"
- "What else?"
- "What else?"
- "Can you explain a little bit about the background of your goal? What would you like to achieve for the team?"

It sometimes happens that previously mentioned goals change in this situation. As facilitator, you can then strike out the point on the flipchart and choose a different formulation.

*Example 6:*   **More or less communication?**

*A German-American team could not agree on their goal: the Americans wanted more communication during a project. The Germans were disturbed in their work by the constant meetings and telephone conferences. So the team coach asked the Americans: "What would be better if you communicated more?" The Americans answered: "We would have more transparency. We would know who is working on what. We would be able to present the project status to our superiors more easily." The team coach then asked the Germans: "What would be better if you had fewer meetings and telephone conferences?" The Germans said: "We would simply get down to business, do our work and could justify the project much more easily to our superiors since something is actually getting done." "I understand," said the team coach, "So everybody wants to know the current project status, who is working on what, and both want to be able to present the pro-*

*ject in a favorable light to their superiors." The group replied: "Yes" and "Ja." That was a goal that both sides could work on. The team coaching ended in agreeing to start an experiment. The team set up a SharePoint site. Every morning each team member entered what he or she was working on and how far they had gotten the day before. The SharePoint site also offered a discussion space in which people could share and discuss their ideas. Both sides put in their slides for the project presentation for their respective managements. Meetings were reduced by half and the experiment proved very successful.*

## Pretend feedback round

Conducting a make-believe feedback round is a very nice way to facilitate goal setting in workshops or team coaching processes. The group pretends it is the last day of the workshop or the process, shortly before everything ends. As usual in workshops, the facilitator asks the group for feedback. Every participant states why they found the workshop especially helpful. The facilitator can visualize the replies on the flipchart – however, this can interrupt the creative flow of

> *In a solution-focused process prioritization is not about deciding on the one and only priority that guarantees success. It is more about thinking about what to start with.*

this method a little bit. You can also simply conduct a fictitious feedback round verbally and then ask every participant to write down their most important points on Post-It notes and stick them onto a flipchart or wall. You can then cluster the Post-It notes and prioritize them if you want. In a solution-focused process, prioritization is not about deciding on the one and only priority that guarantees success. It is more about thinking about what to start with.

## Letter from the future

Participants are asked to choose a future point in time and pretend that they are already there. From that point in time (a positive but realistic future) they write a letter to themselves. This method was introduced into solution-focused consulting by Yvonne Dolan (Dolan, 1991, p. 132). You can use this form of facilitation for goal setting in many different ways:

- Pretend it is the year 20XX and our team coaching process was very successful; everything is just the way you would like it to be. Write a letter to yourself and tell your old self what was useful in the team coaching process. Also tell yourself what has improved and how life is for the team in the year 20XX.

- It is the year 20XX. You've won a prize for the best team, and a newspaper is writing an article about you. Work in small groups and write this article.

- It is the year 20XX. Another team sees how successful you have been and would like to know what you did to make it happen. Work in small groups / in the plenary and describe your success. If you are working in small groups, you can then have half of the small groups interview the other half about how they made this success happen.

*Drawing a picture*

This method is especially useful when you are working with a team of creative people. Participants create a picture of their desired future – either individually or together. Afterwards you create a gallery by hanging up the works of art. If the pictures were created individually, you can ask the "artists" to comment on their work.

More creative methods can be found under "Miracle question".

## Coping questions

In individual coaching, coping questions are used in situations in which the client has little confidence that something can be done in order to improve the situation. It is also used when the client seems very burdened by the problem, and no alternatives or resources are accessible to the client. In individual coaching, you can acknowledge how difficult the problem is and validate the client's perspective of feeling stuck or hopeless. Of course, this is only the beginning. Questions that can help the client regain access to existing exceptions can be sensitive coping questions like, "I can see that this is very difficult; how have you been able to cope?" or, "Under these

*As much as you might understand the team's anger about unfortunate and unchangeable structures and processes, the less it is useful to spend a lot of time talking about things that cannot be changed.*

circumstances, how do you manage to still go to work every morning and do your job well?" How you phrase the question obviously depends on the language the clients use and the general disposition of the clients.

When the team is in a similarly difficult situation, it also helps to think about asking a coping question. There are sometimes difficulties in team coaching that are determined by the environment. For example, you have to adhere to a certain process, use certain software, or collaborate with a specific department. As much as you might understand the team's anger about unfortunate and unchangeable structures and processes, the less it is useful to spend a lot of time talking about things that cannot be changed. Coping questions can help. We first ask whether the topic at hand is something that can be solved or improved today. It is important not to assume anything at this point and try to judge yourself what can and cannot be changed. I experienced situations in which the team was suddenly able to talk about things and change things that I thought could not be changed. For example, when I was meeting with a team of executives for a strategy meeting, they decided to throw out a performance management system that was not doing what it was supposed to, on the spot. However, if the team states that something is set and cannot be changed, it is most helpful to discuss with the team how they can best deal with the situation. It also helps to "normalize" the situation, agree that situations like these happen in other companies, and perhaps share your experiences with other teams in similar situations (obviously without mentioning any names). No organization is perfect. You will always find processes and structures which are difficult for some parts of the organization. This is simply the nature of organizations, and it is helpful for teams to be content with the situation if they know that this is not merely the fault of their own less-than-perfect organization. As a solution-focused team coach, I take the dissatisfaction of the team as engagement and enthusiasm for the success of the organization. Team members want to give their best and be useful for the organization. They are committed in the organization and want to create improvement, even in situations in which improvement is impossible. Acknowledging and respecting their wish for efficiency and success of the organization is usually much appreciated by the team members.

Coping questions happen when they are called for in plenary discussions or when we observe small group discussions. It is not often a planned step in facilitation. There are rarely situations in which it is clear from the beginning that the team has to come to terms with an unchangeable structure. If at all, they happen when two teams are being merged and there are restructurings or layoffs with outplacement. In these cases, it can make sense to reserve a slot in the facilitation for acknowledging the difficulties and expressing appreciation for the resources which the team has already shown in dealing with the difficulties. The following forms of facilitation have shown to be suitable:

### Plenary discussion

You can ask each participant for a contribution in the plenary answering the question: "How have you managed to deal well with the situation?" Depending on the atmosphere and the team, you can then visualize the answers on the flipchart or simply listen to them.

### Work in pairs or small groups

Working in pairs or small groups is another possibility to answer coping questions. One of the difficulties of working in small groups or pairs is the fact that they sometimes (understandably so) ignore the instructions: "Please talk about what you are already doing to deal with the situation. Identify tips and hints that others might also be able to use," and creatively (and sadly less usefully) redefine them to mean: "Talk about all the things that are going wrong, how terribly you are suffering, and why nobody is listening to you, etc." If you are working with pairs or small groups, it is important to be clear with instructions, maybe give a rationale and state why it is not useful to talk about how terrible things are at this point (since this is probably something that people are doing on their own time already quite a lot), but this does not mean that it is not a bad situation or that as a facilitator we want to ignore that it is difficult, but that looking at how people are coping might help the others. During the discussions of the small groups or pairs, it makes sense to keep an eye on what they are doing and redirect the discussions if they are not useful (and sometimes a coping question turns out to be too early and people need the time to vent and have the difficulty acknowledged – but that is very difficult to know in advance.)

## Scaling questions

Scaling questions serve to identify useful differences in individual as well as in team coaching. They are different from objectively measurable key performance indicators or benchmarking data. Solution-focused scaling is not about measuring something objectively. The questions are about helping clients identify relevant differences which can point to more options for solving or improving a situation.

This is how scaling questions work:

1) The scale usually runs from 1 (or 0) to 10. 10 means that the situation has been solved satisfactorily. You can also define 10 as "a time when the problem has vanished" or in another way that is appropriate for the situation. This all depends on the situation and the client. In any case, 10 should be a realistic possibility which can be achieved by the client. A 10 which is not in the sphere of influence of the client, for example, "the outsourcing program has been taken back, and we return to doing the accounting in Germany" would not serve to identify small possible differences in the behavior of the client. This is why scaling

is not used in this way. The first step is therefore the definition of an attractive goal, a 10. Insoo Kim Berg always used a scale of 1-10 because she thought 0 seemed too hopeless. Steve de Shazer was a scientist and preferred to use 0 because the scale does start at 0. There are no studies into what is more effective – why don't you try it out to determine your own preference? Another possibility is to work with the negative scale. Minus 10 means the worst situation and numbers toward 0 or into the positive section of the scale mean a positive difference. The minus scale has the advantage that you can also talk about differences in situations which seem rather hopeless to the client.

2) The next step in asking a scaling question consists of asking the team members to assess the current situation on the scale. It is important to mention that everybody's assessment is completely individual, and the team does not have to agree on a common assessment of the situation. Every team member has his or her own idea of what a 10 is. Some people are more ambitious; others are more realistic. This is why there is no necessity to agree on a common number. For many teams this may sound a bit strange and it is therefore important to mention this before engaging in this step. Otherwise team members can feel offended by the differing assessment of other team members: "What – you think our collaboration is only at a 3? How terrible! How can you!" It is best if the consultant mentions beforehand that nobody can know what the numbers mean exactly for every team member. Finding out what is already working well and what could be next step is important and not the discussion about differing assessments of the current situation.

3) After learning the number of the current situation on the scale, the team coach turns the attention of the team toward what is still working and on the actions of the team that led to the fact that the team is now at an overall point on the scale that is

higher than zero. If most team members are at zero, the team coach can go on with a coping question.

4) The question about a next possible step in the direction of 10 is only asked after what is still working has been explored sufficiently. Questions for the next step are:

- "Which next step in the direction of 10 would you notice?"
- "How would you notice this step?"
- "What will tell you that you are at an X +1?"
- "Who else would notice this step?" (This can be the customers, other teams, the boss of the boss etc. If the team forgets to mention an important stakeholder – oftentimes the customers are not mentioned – the team coach can ask the question directly: "How would the customers notice?"
- "What would relevant stakeholders notice about you that would tell them that you are at an X+1?"
- "What else would you be doing differently after the step you're doing now?"

There are many ways to facilitate scaling questions.

## Scaling walk

The scaling walk illustrates the scale in the physical space. You take one corner of the room to be the 10, the other a 1 or 0. (Katalin Hankovszky lets each person pick a different spot in the room as their 10. This way nobody can know where the others are on their scale.) Participants position themselves physically on the point on the scale at which they see themselves at the moment. The ensuing questions can be accompanied by movements. If you are talking about what is still working or what is going well, you can ask the group to look toward the direction of zero. If you are talking about the effects of a next step, everybody in the group can actually take a step forward. Usually the individual team members are quite distributed on the scale. This way you get natural small groups, who can then discuss the following questions together.

You can use pin boards or flipcharts to visualize. One flipchart could have the heading "what is still / already working well?" and the other "next steps." The flipchart "next steps" is usually quite suitable for clustering and determining areas that need to be talked about to advance a step on the scale.

Exercise 6:    ### Scaling walk for self-coaching

Why don't you try a scaling walk when you are facing a problem by yourself? 10 is somewhere in the room and exemplifies the solution which you want to have. Put yourself on the 10 and contemplate what exactly is different at a 10. Then step onto the point where you are now and think about what tells you that you are already there and not at 0. Then take the next step in the direction of 10: How will you notice that you are one step ahead? Who else will notice and what will tell them?

Example 7:    ### *Scaling walk in training situations*

*A pharmaceutical company had found out that their sales reps were having difficulties talking effectively to "key opinion leaders" – in their case important medical doctors, professors, and heads of research institutes. However, for placing a highly effective new medication, it was important to convince these "key opinion leaders." The new product had many advantages for patients, and the patent for the old medication of the same company would soon expire. There were several sales reps who had successfully argued for changing patients to the new medication – other reps were having more difficulties. The pharmaceutical company therefore wanted to conduct a workshop to increase competence and exchange best practices.*

*We used the scaling walk in the beginning of the workshop. After goal setting, it was clear to everybody why it was so important to push the new medication. The personal targets of the reps were aligned with the company goals, and the incentive structure had been adapted. Every-*

body was also convinced that the new medication offered many advantages for the patients. We had a large room for 25 participants. Everybody positioned themselves on the scale from 1 to 10. 10 was "I like to talk to key opinion leaders about our new product and I know exactly how I can convince them of its usefulness and effectiveness." And 1 was "the opposite." We then asked the participants to form a line and walk from one end of the line (the participants who had no problems talking to key opinion leaders) to the other end of the line (the participants who were less confident of their skills). This way we had small groups of participants who were mixed between more confident and less confident people. There was also one group where everybody was sort of halfway confident (and, of course, the scale only told us about the confidence, not about the actual skills.) These groups of around four people then wrote on Post-It notes what was already working for them. We then clustered the answers on pin boards. It became quite clear that many exchanges of best practices had taken place in the small groups already, and everybody had increased their competence and confidence. Our next question to the same groups was: "How will the key opinion leaders notice that you are one step ahead on the scale?" We also clustered these answers, and it became apparent that there were several topics that could usefully be worked on in small groups. For example, there was one group on "a summary of relevant studies" and one group on "how can I convince people when I know that my medical expertise is far below that of my conversation partners?" And so on.

Although we did not have any deeper knowledge of the subject matter "how to convince key opinion leaders in medicine," we were able to help the participants answer all important questions. Every rep had advanced one or two steps. We were lucky enough to be able to conduct a follow-up day a few weeks later in which participants reflected their experiences together. We also conducted a scaling walk and were very happy to notice that the whole group had significantly moved in the direction of 10. This was also an impressive confirmation for the people who had hired us.

*Plenary discussion with flipchart*

You can also facilitate a scaling question with the whole group using visuals on a flipchart. You take one or two flipcharts and hang them up horizontally. You draw a long line in the middle of the flipcharts and add numbers 0 (or 1) to 10. Yvonne Dolan uses this visualization for the scale in her individual sessions. She draws an arrow instead of the line to signify that even after 10 development is possible. After you have drawn the line on the flipchart, the participants take sticky dots to mark their positions. If you want to have an anonymous process, you can hang up the flipcharts in a different room, behind a pin board, etc. The participants then stick their dots onto the scale during a break when nobody else can see it. The subsequent questions can be asked in the plenary or in small groups.

*Raising your hand*

If you have a very large group and it is not practical for all to move around – be it to the location of the flipcharts or in the form of a scaling walk – you can also ask the participants to indicate their position on the scale through a show of hands. 10 is indicated by raising your hand up as high as possible, and 0 is lowering your hand as far as possible.

*Humming*

If you are working with large groups and on topics that make it difficult for participants to be open about their assessment, you can ask the participants to start humming when you call out a given number. Humming is not as obvious as raising your hand and the whole process is usually fun and lightens the mood.

## Exceptions and resources

There are many possibilities for asking the team about exceptions and resources. You identify exceptions and resources by talking about times when the problem did not occur as intensively or when something went better than was expected. This way the team can gain confidence that the situation can improve. By analyzing the exceptions to the problem or the instances in which the situation was a little bit like the way the team would like it to be, the team often comes up with strategies which have been successful and promise to be successful in the future.

A good time for asking about exceptions and resources is after a scaling question – or during a scaling process. You can use questions like: "When did you have a time where it was a little bit better?" or "What kind of situations did you have that were higher on the scale than you are now?" Afterwards you can ask: "What was your contribution? What did you do to make that happen?" to identify possible alternatives for the team.

If there are several exceptions, you can ask the team to split into small groups and determine what made the exception possible and what their contribution was. In our experience it makes sense to write down the question, "What was your contribution?" or "What did the exception enable you to do differently?" on the flipchart that the participants will use to record their findings or distribute a handout with the questions. Without written instructions the discussion might revert to talking about why the exception is not the norm (and that would not be very helpful at this moment).

You can also connect appreciative feedback with the search for exceptions and resources. You ask the group to identify a "highlight" or "sparkling moment" and invite them to talk about who in the group contributed to it. Nobody is allowed to talk about themselves. Everybody shares their positive observations of what other people have contributed. If this seems too artificial or embarrassing, you can also ask the group to note the observations on Post-It notes and stick them to a flipchart or wall. This way, however, you run the risk that you have somebody whose contributions are forgotten and this might be hurtful to that person. To avoid this you can ask everybody to write one Post-It note for each of the other participants. To ease the logistics, you can also prepare Post-It notes with the names of the participants on them. In our experience simply talking about each other's contribution is easiest (at least in central Europe).

## Miracle question

Coert Visser (http://solutionfocusedchange.blogspot.com/2007/10/who-invented-miracle-question.html) tells the story of how Insoo Kim Berg developed the miracle question by accident in a conversation with a client. He quotes Steve de Shazer in an interview from 1996 (http://www.sfwork.com/jsp/index.jsp?lnk=618) which was conducted by Harry Norman, Mark McKergow and Jenny Clarke:

> "The Miracle Question evolved out of one day Insoo asked a question and the answer was, "Oh it would take a miracle!" and Insoo said "Well, ye, suppose... suppose a miracle did happen"... and that started the whole thing. The answer was pretty nice, whatever it was. The answer was nice, so almost all our stuff like that is invented by clients first."

The miracle question was subsequently developed further at the Brief Therapy Center. In 1988 it was first published by Steve de Shazer (1988, p. 5-6).

*In the miracle question you do not assume a linear connection between problem and solution. You focus on what the world would look like if the problem or challenge had disappeared.*

It invites clients to imagine a world in which the problem or challenge no longer exists. Clients explore observable differences in that situation and possible approaches for first changes for the better. There is a difference between the miracle question and goal setting questions. In the miracle question, you do not assume a linear connection between problem and solution. You focus on what the world would look like if the problem or challenge had disappeared. This draws the attention of the clients to what happens outside the problem. The question is oftentimes completely against our first impulse to want to understand the problem in as much detail as possible in order to be able to find a solution.

There are many ways of usefully posing the miracle question. Here is a standard variant:

*"I would like to ask you question. It is a little bit strange and requires some imagination."*

*"Suppose our workshop/conversation is over and you go home. At home you do all the things that you usually do in the evening. Maybe you'll have some dinner, watch television, brush your teeth ... and then sometime that evening you get tired and go to sleep. And while you are fast asleep, in the middle of the night, a miracle happens, just like that. And the miracle is that everything that we have been talking about and maybe even what we haven't talked about has been solved, just like that. Now you are fast asleep, and that is why you do not realize, that a miracle happened. The next morning nobody is telling you about the miracle either. How are you going to start noticing in the morning that a miracle happened?"*

Oftentimes teams do not know what to answer right away. The consultant can make it easier by asking a few follow-up questions:

*"What would be a first small sign?"*

*"What else?"*

People then usually start to smile and find answers that range from the trivial to the important. The team coach takes care to get a rich description of the differences after the miracle that can serve to identify well-formulated goals and small observable differences and possible steps afterwards. How are the team members going to notice? What is everybody doing differently after the miracle? What are observable, interactional signs that the miracle has happened? Perspective change questions (e.g. "How are other people going to notice?"), sometimes called circular questions in systemic consulting, can be useful to help the team generate answers that draw it forward:

*"How will your customers notice that the miracle happened for you?"*

*"What would others say was your contribution to the miracle picture?"*

*"How will your family notice?"*

Asking about an outside perspective serves to identify observable differences, just like when you are working on goals. We only imagine the outside perspectives – what the others will actually notice is and stays unknown. There is a similarity to the "circular questions" in systemic therapy. The difference in solution-focused consulting is the fact that integrating an imagined outside perspective only serves to identify observable differences. In systemic consulting, these questions are sometimes used to uncover circular processes and patterns of relationships in order to gain greater clarity on the interwoven patterns of interactions or collect other information (Reich, 2008).

*In solution-focused consulting, integrating an imagined outside perspective only serves to identify observable differences.*

Peter de Jong and Insoo Kim Berg suggest the following structure for posing the miracle question in their book "Interviewing for Solutions" (1998):

- Start slowly and tentatively
- Mark the question as unusual or strange
- Start in future tense or conditional: "How would you notice?"
- When you are asking about observable signs in follow-up questions after the miracle question, change to the indicative: "When the miracle happens, you…"
- Gently and persistently confirm the team's change of attention to what will be different when the team is starting to revert to describing the problem (which also has its place, but not here)

Some people think that it is difficult to pose a traditional miracle question in the context of companies and corporations. They presume that clients think the question frivolous or silly. In our experience, the miracle question works well in an organizational context. In 15 years it has only happened once that a participant refused to answer it because "it is too new agey." And even in this situation, we think that the reason was probably more that the participant was not interested much in developing solutions at all. We should have probably realized this earlier and should have refrained from asking him the miracle question – but hindsight is always 20/20. Steve de Shazer once said if you want to pose the miracle question, you should take care to prepare the ground, just like when you want to broil a steak the frying pan needs to be hot. Steve did not say much about what exactly "preparing the ground" meant for him here. We presume that the client's willingness to search for a solution is probably part of it.

If you don't feel comfortable asking the miracle question in its traditional form in an organizational context, you can also experiment with other formats. The crucial element is that the linear connection between problem and solution is dissolved – independent of the question that you use. The world after the miracle makes things possible which would not be possible without a miracle. So instead of speaking about miracle you can also ask about "an unforeseeable development".

Example 8:     **Strategy meeting**

> The board of trustees of a charitable organization had hired a full time manager for their free advisory centers. Previously, the daily business had been run by the Board of Trustees themselves, which had taken a lot of time and energy. On the one hand, the six board members were happy that they no longer had to be involved in the daily business. On the other hand, they felt very connected to the advisory centers, in which two of the board members also worked as consultants. These two had insisted on hiring a manager because they wanted to spend their time consulting and helping people rather than drawing up personnel plans, remuneration structures, and dealing with taxes. The team wanted to become clear on how to work together as a "Board of Trustees without operative responsibilities" to the benefit of the association.
>
> We asked everybody to leave the room and then installed an imaginary "time and miracle shower" in the door. Everybody re-entered the room and convened a session two years after a full-time manager had been established successfully. Like in almost any follow-up facilitation, we started with: "What is better?" Contributions were: "We have been able to work strategically again. We started a new project and have been able to do more lobbying for our clientele, and so on." The next

*question was: "What have you done to make this success possible?" The group stated: "We maintained strong contact with our manager. We had regular meetings and agreed on a concept on who decides what and when." These answers also partially determined the further content of the meeting with the Board. For example, it had become clear that it would be crucial for success to have clear guidelines and structures for decisions. We worked on a suggestion for these guidelines afterwards.*

## Facilitation techniques

There are many different ways to facilitate the miracle question in a team coaching process. It is important to take care that the description of the miracle of each team member remains uncontested and everybody's perspective is acknowledged. If there are contradictory descriptions, the team coach might ask: "So, if this part of the miracle happens for you, what will be better?" Usually what looks like a contradictory description at first glance then dissolves into a picture that can be shared by all. The same is true for answers that seem silly at first.

*Example 9:* **The Russian countess**

*We were once consulting with the management team of a large Eastern-European luxury hotel in a mixture between a strategy session and a management team building event. We had asked a traditional miracle question and the group was working on it in small groups writing their answers on a flipchart. The atmosphere was relaxed and happy, and you could assume from the laughter that was audible behind the flipcharts that the groups were having fun answering the question. The main reason for the mirth became apparent in the ensuing plenary discussion: Two out of three groups had described the following story as part of their miracle: "Countess XY is no longer sitting at the bar starting at five o'clock every day, drunk and bothering our international clients." Of course, this is not a well-formulated goal. It is specific and realistic, but it is stated negatively and not really in the influence of the hotel management. We asked the group: "So if Countess XY is no longer sitting at the bar, drunk, what is better?" The group generated answers like: "We could offer a professional bar service," "The international consulting companies could use our bar as a meeting point after work," "These companies then might also choose our hotel to host their guests or conferences." We could work on the goals stated in these answers irrespective of the presence or absence of Countess XY – which turned out not to be the decisive factor after all.*

## Small groups or plenary

If you encourage the group to work on the miracle questions in small groups, you have the advantage that everybody can describe his or her miracle. On the other hand, it is also very useful for the team when they hear how every team member imagines a positive future for the team. It becomes apparent that every team member wants to imagine a positive development and is therefore also likely engaged in creating it. A positive image that the team members have of each other is created

*Asking the miracle question in the plenary can create or support a positive image that the team members have of each other.*

or supported, which in turn is very useful for the further process. Depending on the group size, you can decide what is more important: giving each individual team member time and space to discuss a personal miracle, or sharing the miracle in the plenary. In doubt, we would tend to ask the miracle question in the plenary with the larger group. Another alternative is asking the team members to jot down bullet points describing their day after the miracle individually for five or ten minutes. These bullet points are then shared afterwards in the plenary. You can also apply Post-It notes to the individual work asking everybody to use black markers and write only one point per Post-It note. You can then use a wall chart or flipchart to cluster and visualize the answers to the miracle question.

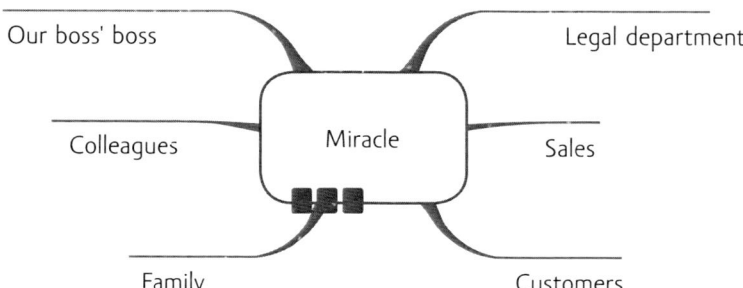

Another possibility is asking the follow-up questions to the miracle question one after the other. You start with: "How are you going to start realizing that the miracle has happened?" and ask the participants to write down their answers on Post-It notes. You then asked the plenary: "Who else will notice that the miracle has happened?" You can then create a mind map on a flipchart where each individual branch is a person or group of people who will notice that a miracle happened.

You then create small groups which each work on the signs that will tell one stakeholder group that the miracle must have happened. One group might work on what their families might notice, the other might work on what their colleagues will notice, and the next might work on what the legal department will notice. They all collect their answers on flipcharts (or pieces of flipchart paper if you do not have enough flipcharts). These flipcharts are then hung up on the wall and are read by everybody. Usually many answers are created which makes it necessary to start a process of prioritization. This can be facilitated by using sticky dots or votes. Scaling is also a relatively simple way to prioritize the answers. For each flipchart you could ask: "On a scale of 0-10, where 10 is the morning your stakeholder groups realize that the miracle must have happened and zero is the opposite, where are you now? What is already working well? What would be a next small step?"

## Miracle Board

There are many creative ways to facilitate the miracle question. It is fun to describe a desired future together, and this mood can also influence the method of facilitation. When you're working with a "Miracle board," you draw three lines on the flipchart to create six spaces which are then used to create "scenes" or "pictures." Small groups or individuals start by drawing the last image: the morning after the miracle. It is very useful to give the instruction that the image should show the team acting, doing something the morning after the miracle – otherwise you run the risk that the description of the future has nothing to do with the daily reality that the team desires after the miracle, e.g. we all won the lottery, the aliens have landed and have solved all our problems. The pictures before the last picture should show moments which are a bit like being on the way to the miracle situation. The first image should be a real incident from the team's past that was like the miracle, such as a "forerunner" of the miracle. After drawing the flipcharts, they are hung up in the room and the participants have time to look at them. Afterwards you can move on to scaling.

## Role-play in the future / videos

The basic idea of the "Miracle board" is that team members create a rich and vivid image of the desired future and then go back to the first sign of the miracle that happened in the past. This basic idea can also be implemented with other media. The participants can role-play significant moments or shoot short video sequences. Especially when you are working on a strategic new orientation or when there have been significant changes in the team, this method can be really useful to store the results of the miracle question as videos and keep them accessible for a while (e.g. on a shared server or hard drive). Technically this has become rather easy – most participants use smartphones which are capable of recording short video sequences with a sufficient quality. Apple, as well as Microsoft computers, usually come with free programs that you can use to edit the videos (e.g. Microsoft Movie Maker).

## Pin board-timeline

I once developed a really simple visualization of the miracle question for a workshop. The basic idea is the "timeline." Create a long stretch of flipchart paper on the wall by gluing four or five flipcharts together at the short end. Start with the description of the miracle at the end of the timeline. Everybody can jot down the most important elements of their miracle with markers on Post-It notes and stick them onto the last flipchart labelled "miracle." When you are facilitating this, take care to ask about concrete signs of the miracle: "How will you notice that a miracle has happened?" In larger groups you can also assign different perspectives; for example, part of the group describes how the customers will notice that a miracle has happened, and the other part describes how top management will notice it, etc. The different perspectives can be visualized by differently colored Post-It notes. After sticking the miracle Post-It notes to the end of the timeline, you can work back to the present and describe the incidents in which signs of the miracle are apparent. You can also reserve one or two flipcharts for the past where the group is invited to write down incidents that already were a little bit like after the miracle; this gives them confidence that it is possible for the team to take steps in the direction of the miracle.

## A fictitious meeting

Holding a fictitious meeting in the future is a shorter way of facilitating the miracle question. The team imagines the miracle has happened and they are holding the meeting in the future. The team members can either play themselves in the future and talk about what they appreciate about the new situation, or they can take the roles of important stakeholders and reflect on the wonderful development of the team from an outside perspective. The latter variant is very useful for strategy development processes. It is also quite useful to take care that the answers are somewhat realistic. Visualizing the fictitious meeting in the future is a little bit difficult – you can record the meeting on video or audio and then summarize or visualize afterwards, but this is a lot of work, takes time, and the answers are not available immediately. Another possibility is asking an assistant to jot down the most important points on the flipchart or with Post-It notes. On occasion, I have simply recorded the most important contributions by typing them quickly into my computer and sorting them later with the group by showing them via data projector.

### Going for a walk

Sending the participants for a walk in groups of two or three is very simple way of facilitating the miracle question. Most often participants appreciate being able to get up and move. Often when you go for a walk, you also have more creative ideas than when you are stuck in a conference room. For visualization, ask the group to take markers and Post-It notes, or simply ask people to report on their ideas and write them down on the flipchart when the group returns.

# Small steps

Having agreed upon concrete actions and to-do lists in the time after the workshop is a sign of success to many of our customers. In solution-focused therapy, the therapist usually leaves the follow-up and choice of the small steps in the hands of the client. This is the same in solution-focused team coaching. The team chooses appropriate steps which will lead it in the direction of its goal. The facilitator's role here is to help the team make decisions and document them. There is a small gradual difference to solution-focused therapy or solution- focused individual coaching. In solution- focused individual coaching, we would usually not write down or visualize the steps the client wants to take. We would probably leave this to the client. Visualizing agreed actions for the team, however, generates more commitment and fits well with the culture of many teams.

### Decision-making

It is quite useful to make sure as facilitator that the people who are given action points or to-dos by the team are also willing and happy to take them on and that the team leader agrees. It is important to clarify within the team coaching process what can be decided by whom (you can find more about this in the section on clarifying the contract.) If it is not clear whether a possible decision is within the power of the people present, it is better to err on the side of caution and ask or give the team the task of asking whether this is within the scope of their decision making power. Otherwise it can be really frustrating if the team decides upon measures which cannot be carried out due to overarching concerns. The same is true for decisions about the use of resources: the owners of these resources need to agree or be asked to agree. For example, the team can think that hiring an intern would solve many of their problems and may start planning steps to get there. If there is a company wide hiring freeze, this will not help. This is the same with travel arrangements or projects which tie up hours of your own or in other teams.

## *Prioritizing*

Creative teams sometimes generate a plethora of ideas for possible actions. Of course, every suggestion is welcome as an idea. However, you can sometimes not implement everything that is being suggested. The facilitator is asked to help the team prioritize. We use traditional tools for prioritizing although, of course, we know that it is never completely discernible which action will have the greatest success. On the other hand, you have to somehow agree on what you will try first. It is best to leave the choice of prioritization method to the group. For that it is quite useful if you can explain ideas to them in a short and sweet manner.

## Eisenhower-Matrix

You create a matrix or a four-field diagram of "important – not important" and "urgent – not urgent" and ask the team to assign every suggested action to a space in this matrix. Visualization on a flipchart using Post-It notes is quite practical.

| Urgent and important | Not urgent and important |
| --- | --- |
| | |
| Not important and urgent | Not urgent and not important |
| | |

## Short-term / Long-term

You can also sort the suggestions by determining whether they can be implemented quickly and promise short-term success (quick wins) or take more time but might have a lot of impact.

## Voting

Asking the group to vote on which steps to take first is a very quick way of prioritizing action points. In order to prevent a situation in which someone is unable to identify with the result because none of their suggestions were voted in, you can give every team member more than one vote per suggestion. You can visualize that by giving every team member a number of sticky dots.

## Individual tasks / homework / experiments

If the action points are something that can be worked on individually and assigning specific tasks with due dates and resources is not workable (e.g. when the topic is "creating a better work atmosphere" or "showing more appreciation for each other"), you can ask each individual team member to state what they would like to "start doing" or "do more of" in the future. (In some team coaching sessions, participants are also asked about what they would like to stop doing. Solution-focused team coaching can do without that question since for us it is about what needs to happen rather than what people need to stop doing.) After telling each other what they would like to start doing or do more of, team members can write down their actions on the flipchart or the facilitator can take on that task. You can also facilitate this step by asking everybody to write their actions on index cards so they can take them back to their offices as a reminder.

## Peter Szabo's implementation interviews

At the 2012 SOL world conference in Oxford, Peter Szabo demonstrated a nice method which can contribute to people actually implementing what they planned. This method is especially suitable when the implementation plan focuses on things you know you should really start doing but that somehow just do not happen.

To begin, every team member answers two questions which are written down on two different pieces of paper:

> Question 1: What would you like to implement in the near future?
>
> Question 2: Tell a story about time where you managed to implement or started doing something that wasn't easy at first.

The group then pairs up. In the first round, both partners tell each other their success stories without mentioning their implementation project from question one. After the partners have finished telling their success stories, they tell each other what was helpful or inspiring about the other partner's story.

In the next step everybody finds a new partner. First, one of the two reports his or her implementation project. The other partner answers: "I don't know if this has anything to do with your project, but I have a story for you."

He or she then tells the success story that his or her previous partner shared in the previous round. If he or she knows anyone in the group who has a similar story or can share hints that could help with implementation, he or she refers the partner to that person.

The partners then switch roles.

In the end both exchange what they learned from these conversations and how this supports them in actually implementing what they planned.

## Confidence, benefits and appreciative feedback

Asking about how confident participants are that the measures they agreed upon (or the results of their team coaching) will lead to the desired improvement is another important element in solution-focused team coaching. When we ask this question, we are sometimes surprised about the answers. As consultants, we might be very confident that the group identified action items that would lead them to success, but the group or parts of the group might not

*In solution-focused coaching we don't assume that there are participants with a "hidden agenda." Of course, we know that "hidden agendas" exist, but we don't pay much attention to them.*

be at all confident. It is best not to overcomplicate situations like these by starting a process of interpretation about how this occurred, for example by assuming that there are "hidden agendas." Of course, we know that things like "hidden agendas" exist, but we do not pay much attention to them. We try to create a framework in which everything that can serve to improve the situation can be stated in a respectful way.

Creating this framework also includes asking people that seem distant or not engaged what can be done to make it possible for them to join in. Sadly enough there are groups which have already had to experience several processes for development or even coaching processes that were not useful. Their confidence that something can be changed by engaging in such a process is understandably very low. They have learned that they have to play along in order not to create any negative attention, but they do not believe that anything will change. Asking such groups how confident they are that something can change – either in the beginning or at the end of the workshop – can be very useful. If the answer is: "We are not very confident", then we deal with the situation as if we had asked a scaling question. We ask what, if anything, gives them at least a little bit of confidence and then go on to ask what needs to happen so they can have more confidence that a positive change is possible.

*Example 10:* **A useless presentation coaching**

*A large supplier of automotive parts asked us to offer a presentation coaching to a few of their important employees. The participants were technical specialists and middle managers. They were all between 30 and 40 years old, motivated and friendly. Our feeling was that the coaching was going very well and that everybody had made a lot of progress in their presentation skills. At the end of the first day, we asked them how useful this had been for them and how confident they were that they could use what they had learned. We fully expected enthusiastic answers. You can imagine how surprised we were when we heard that the partici-pants had really enjoyed themselves but that they had no confidence that they could use any of these skills in their daily lives.*

*Whenever a team member notices that somebody has carried out a task or is behaving in a positive way, they secretly put a small sign (e.g. a paper flower, a glass gem, etc.) on the desk of the person who has acted in the desired way.*

*Quite flustered, we asked if there was something that was at least a little bit useful and much to our dismay we received no answer. Of course, we were not able to hide our disappointment. The participants must have felt sorry for us and said that this was not our fault, but that the presentations they were used to giving were based on a very different procedure. In their presentations they were only using the so-called "one-pager," a presentation with only one slide that contained all the necessary information. Most presentations happened over the telephone or in meeting rooms where everybody was sitting down. Our wonderful exercises and coaching conversations on structuring and de-signing PowerPoint presentations, on dealing with stage fright and exuding confidence, were very interesting but not applicable in their organization. In this moment we realized that we should have been more thorough in our contract negotiation with the learning and development department and also with the group. We believed that we knew what a business presentation is – and thinking you know is almost always a mistake. Had we been more thorough in our approach and practiced solution-focused "not knowing," we would have been more to the point with our presentation coaching. Luckily we had asked the question about the confidence and usefulness in the middle of the coaching. We could therefore use the second day to work on "one pagers" and the presentation situations described by our participants.*

## Confidence scale

You can use a confidence scale with groups just as with individuals. You ask about what makes the team confident that change will happen and what could make the team even a little bit more confident. The question works exactly like a scaling question and can be facilitated the same way. If you scale confidence at the end of the workshop, you usually do not have a lot of time left so that working in the plenary is the most practical way of facilitation. The more time you have after the confidence scale, the longer forms of facilitation you can use because you can work with the team's answers afterwards.

## Confidence snowball fight

The confidence snowball fight was described by a solution-focused colleague on Facebook. He had finished the team coaching process with a group, and many useful changes had been achieved. The last workshop in this longer process took place in a cold and very snowy winter. The colleague asked the group to write down everything that makes them confident that the progress which they had achieved could be maintained or even built upon on pieces of white Xerox paper, one comment per sheet. The participants wrote their answers, crushed the papers into paper snowballs, and had a very fun snowball fight. After a while everybody collected the snowballs lying around. Everybody read the comments on the snowballs that they had collected out loud.

## Positive paranoia

Ben Furman and Tapani Ahola coined the term "positive paranoia" for this hope and confidence generating experiment. The background for this experiment is that teams and other groups like to focus on what does not work and overlook all the positive things that are already leading them in the desired direction. Ben Furman and Tapani Ahola work with teams to the point at which the desired goal is clear and well-formulated, and they have hope and have identified first steps. They do not create a large action plan or follow-up plan because that way you risk that somebody does not do what they promised to do and then the attention of the team reverts to focusing on what is not working. Instead, the team receives the task of observing closely what is already going into the right direction. Whenever a team member notices that somebody has carried out a task or is behaving in a positive way, they secretly put a small sign (e.g. a paper flower, a glass gem, etc.) on the desk of the person who has acted in the desired way. This experiment sounds a little bit silly and it might remind people of the little pictures or bonus stars that their elementary school teacher used to indicate that they had done their homework well. However, what is important here is focusing the attention of the team on what is working – whichever way you manage to that. It is well worth thinking about what could be a way of establishing this direction of observation for the team that is in keeping with the team's culture. One idea that we have used was not to use gems, stars or flowers but use coffee tokens for the cafeteria.

## Resource gossip of the consultants

When you are working with a team of consultants, you can use "resource gossip" to give appreciative feedback to the team and increase their confidence for the possibility of change. The group of consultants pretends to be gossiping about their observations of the team while the team is listening. Of course, this is not the usual gossip, but resource gossip. Therefore, the consultants talk about all the things they have observed that make them confident that the team will reach its goal. You can do this live or even in teleconferences where the consultants are talking and the team is listening in. If possible and useful, you can also involve other stakeholders to listen in on or share their observations of the changes in that conversation; for example, customers or other departments that the team works with.

*Atmosphere / benefit diagram*

The perceived benefit of the team coaching process and the confidence that it will have positive results for the team are closely connected. We therefore like to ask the team how useful they think the process has been long before the end of the process. On the one hand, this helps us to correct things that might have gone wrong. On the other hand, the team feels strengthened in their ability to control the process and be taken seriously. We usually create a flipchart with a matrix. One axis is labelled "benefit" and the other is labelled "work atmosphere." Participants can anonymously make a cross at the appropriate point for them, at the point where they see the process at the moment. We then ask what has already been useful or beneficial and what was good about the work atmosphere. We take care not to just fish for compliments for us as facilitators, but to invite the team to observe what they have contributed to the benefit and positive atmosphere of the process. Obviously, we also ask what if anything could be done to improve both.

# Other workshop formats

*Reflecting team*

The solution-focused reflecting team is a format for discussing cases among colleagues. It is based on Tom Andersen (1991) and was further developed by Harry Norman. Liselotte Baejaert and Anton Stellamans (2012) also have a similar process called "O.A.S.I.S" in their book on resilience. Other than more traditional forms of supervision or "intervision," the solution-focused reflecting team does without the construction of hypotheses or talking about resonances or transference and counter-transference. The solution-focused reflecting team serves to generate ideas to help the person who has a case he or she wants to discuss.

The solution-focused reflecting team can be carried out in a group of 4 to 12 people. There is a facilitator, a timekeeper (in small groups one person can take both roles) and the person with the issue or case. The other participants act as coaches or consultants for the person with the case.

We carry out the reflecting team in the following structure:

1. At the beginning, everybody is sitting in a circle. The "case-donor" – the person with the issue – describes their goal for the process. The facilitator poses solution-focused questions to clarify the goal: "What should be different after our consulting process?" "On a scale of 1-10, where are you now?" "What have you tried already that has worked a little bit?" etc. This step is carried out until the goal seems sufficiently clear (4-5 minutes).

2. Participants can ask clarification questions about the issue. It is important that the facilitator gently insists that these clarification questions do not contain secret suggestions. "Why haven't you thought about doing..." is not a clarification question (4-5 minutes).

3. The "case donor" then turns around so that he or she is sitting with his or her back to the group. He or she shouldn't be able to interact with the group verbally or nonverbally. The group then takes turns expressing appreciative statements about what impresses them with what the "case donor" has already tried. They mention everything that makes them confident that the "case donor" will reach his or her goal. This phase aims at enabling the "case donor" to listen to the suggestions and ideas of the group and make him or her confident that his or her issue can be solved (4-5 minutes).

4. In the next round, everybody can offer their ideas, suggestions, and own experiences to the "case donor," who is still sitting with his or her back to the group. This can be an effective brainstorming if everybody chips in or conducts themselves in a structured way with people taking turns in the order that they

are seated. You can ask everybody to jot down their ideas on pieces of paper first before they share them with the group. This way you get a larger variety of ideas. The "case donor" writes down everything that seems useful for him or her (10 minutes).

5.  The "case donor" can then turn around and tell the group what was useful for him or her and thank the group if he or she wants to (2 minutes).

You can also take a break in phase 4 and ask the "case donor" whether what is being discussed with the group is going into the right direction, or whether there is a new question that has developed that the "case donor" would like to ask. This way the "case donor" gets the opportunity to be more concrete about the ideas that he or she wants the group to generate.

## Tetralemma

Matthias Varga von Kibéd and Insa Sparrer developed an interesting possibility to work with teams who are confronted with having to take a decision, the tetralemma (Varga von Kibéd & Sparrer, 2005). It is derived from Indian logic and focuses on solving the perception of a dilemma with two diametrical poles (e.g. taking on a project – not taking on a project) and generating more than these two possibilities. Here is our variant of working with the tetralemma:

We create a constellation of 5 different positions:

1.  the one
2.  the other
3.  both
4.  neither of the two
5.  the fifth non-position "none of this but also not this""

Each corner of the room can represent one of the four positions marked by a flipchart, a piece of paper on the floor, or other markers. The team first walks into the first corner and describes, for example, why they absolutely want to take on the project (the one), what the advantages are and who would profit. Then everybody moves to the opposite corner and describes (the other): why the project should definitely not be taken on, what are the disadvantages, and who would benefit. On the third position in yet another corner, the team members look at "the one" and "the other" and reflect on what "both" could mean: in our case, for example, the things that are important to the team irrespective of what they decide, being able to manage their daily priorities professionally, and looking good in front of other departments. On the fourth position, "neither of the two," the team looks at all the other three positions. The team might think about alternatives that would also achieve the goals that became apparent on position three: taking on a different project, describing the successes of the team, the company blog, etc. The fifth non-position is not a position in the room. The team walks around together and reflects on what else all of this might mean. On the fifth position you often develop interesting conversations and insights far beyond the solution of the issues at hand.

If there is no room, you can also use a flipchart to draw the different positions, use toy figurines or take four chairs and ask one person to sit down on each chair as a representative for the respective position. The fifth element stays standing and can walk around. The representatives of the positions on the chairs talk from their positions and the rest of the team listens. Afterwards the team summarizes what were the most important and most interesting insights that came up in the discussion.

### Turning other team coaching exercises into solution-focused exercises

Most traditional team coaching exercises can be turned into effective solution-focused intervention by using a few hints and tricks (which we describe below). Before describing how we can turn other team coaching exercises into solution- focused exercises, we would like to mention a few words of caution. Every once in a while we have come across exercises whose background is so different from solution-focused ideas that they cannot be turned into a solution-focused team coaching exercise at all. Here are a few kinds of exercises in which even a miracle during the night would not work.

## What is not suitable?

Solution-focused approaches to team coaching are always resource oriented. It is about helping participants to discover strengths and possibilities, resources they (no longer) were aware of. After a solution-focused task, participants are positively surprised about themselves – be it because of the content they discovered or because learning was fun and easy. The good working relationship between coach and participants is a result of this dynamic. In a few older coaching concepts you still find exercises which aim at demonstrating the teams' incompetence in order to strengthen their motivation to learn. For example, in a train-the-trainer session for team trainers that we once participated in, the trainer established the rule that from now on all decisions of the group would have to be 100% consensual. The aim of this rule was to demonstrate to the team that consensual decisions are very difficult and almost impossible. As was to be expected, the group got stuck in very frustrating discussions and wasn't even able to agree on when to take breaks. Afterwards, the trainer elaborated on the reasons for this failure. Most participants had already experienced such situations before, so there was not much information gained. The frustration level was immense, and the team's relationship to the trainer was so disturbed that a few participants left after this exercise. If there is one advantage of demonstrating incompetence, it is the clarity with which a problem appears (or put facetiously: is created). We think that this clarity can be achieved much more easily without disturbing the working atmosphere and thereby the willingness of the participants to change or learn.

*Most traditional team coaching exercises can be turned into an effective solution-focused intervention by using a few hints and tricks*

A solution-focused approach creates a good working relationship between coach (or facilitator, trainer) and participants quickly. It also consciously helps construct positive and supportive relationships between the participants. Exercises which endanger these working relationships are hard to turn into solution-focused exercises. All coaching components which produce conflicts or serve to make one participant lose face also fall into that category. In one team coaching, for example, a participant always came in late after breaks. The other participants tolerated his behavior. It was only when the coach mentioned this phenomenon that the group learned that the participant had been instructed by the coach to be late in order to be able to demonstrate the dynamic of unpunctual starts. The goal of such interventions is often to show what is "really going on" in the team. The root cause of the problem needs to be identified and eradicated once and for all. There is a clear linear causality between "the problem" (and the team member who is seen as the problem) and solution (which is usually getting rid of the problem). In solution-focused team coaching, the goal of the intervention would be elicited differently: by asking the miracle question, exploring exceptions from the problem or resources of the team and defining small steps into the direction of the goal.

Similar ideas also form the basis of so-called "instruments" for team diagnostics or personality diagnostics or personality typologies. The team has a problem. The team coach therefore starts looking for the root cause (more or less scientifically): all team members fill in a questionnaire to determine their personality type, for example the DISC profile, the Myers-Briggs-Type-Indicator, their team roles, etc. The results show where to find the real problem of the team and how it might be solved, for example by adding another team member with a complementary personality type. These kinds of interventions are especially difficult to combine with a solution-focused approach when the instruments applied are not taken as typologies (like DISC or Myers-Briggs) but are misunderstood as diagnoses of static personality characteristics. The solution-focused approach assumes that change always happens – it is therefore difficult for us to work with instruments which posit unchangeable personality cores.

For solution-focused team coach, working with personality profiles looks like a detour via a presumed root cause of the problem. However, it is still possible to follow-up such an intervention in a solution-focused way. You might ask: "What does the typology analysis show are the advantages and resources of your team?", "Where do these resources show up in your daily life?", "If you assume that XYZ is missing from your team – how have you been able to cope?", "On a scale of 1-10, where you with regard to..." This way, the personality diagnostics can provide a useful invitation for a conversation in the team or individual coaching.

Another word of warning: some typologies like for example "Integral Coaching" or "Spiral Dynamics" (Ken Wilber) assign a development level to each client. There is a globally determined path of development, almost like a path to salvation, and the desired development of the client or the team is predetermined. Assuming a predetermined, globally and eternally valid path for development for every person is a philosophical or religious stance that you can take – however, it is very far from assuming that every case is different, that you work on what your client wants. In solution-focused coaching we elicit the goals of the clients and do not assume that they pre-exist somewhere.

When we are working with colleagues who come from approaches which seem incompatible to our view of coaching, we try to acknowledge their good intentions to be helpful to their clients. Someone who represents "Spiral Dynamics" or Jungian personality types is not a bad coach or worse, a bad person. He or she might be helpful, yet not solution-focused. Especially when working with human resource departments, we have often experienced that a fruitful collaboration is possible even when consultants espouse different approaches when you accept the differences and are curious about them.

## What is suitable?
Many traditional exercises and team coaching tools can be used for a solution-focused learning or change process: exercises from outdoor training, games or team exercises suitable for a seminar room, structured role plays, exercises with observer feedback, etc.

## Strategies for transformation
There are basically two ways of turning exercises and tools into solution-focused exercises: You can start from

*There are basically two ways of turning exercises and tools into solution focused exercises: you can start from the solution- focused process and enrich its elements with exercises, or you can take exercises which you know from a different context and turn them into solution-focused exercises.*

the solution-focused process and enrich its elements with exercises, or you can take exercises, which you know from a different context, and turn them into solution-focused exercises.

If you want to change an exercise in a solution-focused way, it makes sense to look at the different phases of the exercise: What do you need to take care of when you are introducing the exercise, when you are carrying it out and when you are debriefing it so that the exercise can be useful for the clients.

## Introduction / Briefing

There are a few general success factors for introducing team activities, for example, clarifying the goal of the exercise so that participants feel safe and convinced that it is a good use of their time or announcing the structure and timing of the activity. Here are a few additional hints for directing the focus of participants on resources and success factors when using activities in a solution-focused way.

When you are introducing the activity, you can ask the whole group or individual participants to observe what is already going well during the activity. You can distribute observer sheets or assign targeted observation tasks focusing on individual factors in order to get useful and positive feedback. It is about identifying what works and not about identifying what does not work. Of course, we still know that the context of an activity is very different from the context of daily work. However, if something goes well in an activity, it can be a first small sign that this is also possible in the daily life of the team.

## Delivery

When the activity is carried out, every team member should feel safe. Nobody should have to fear to be embarrassed or lose face. Of course, as a team coach this is not always completely under your control. Sometimes you have obnoxious participants, who like ridiculing others. In this case it is important to de-escalate the situation. If you want to talk about it, you should be able to appreciate everybody's perspective but also show that a different way of communicating has better results for the team atmosphere.

*Example 11:* **Welcome to the jungle**

> *I was conducting the team coaching with a group of trainees. Among them was a girl who did not seem very popular. Whenever she said something, two other trainees were rolling their eyes. The exercise was about finding a path through a grid marked on the floor as a team as quickly as possible. In order to protect the unpopular girl and create a better atmosphere for learning for everybody I was looking for a way to busy the eye rolling trainees so that they would no longer have time to put down or complain about the girl. I decided to give them the role of referee which did not leave any time for them to do anything else.*

## Debriefing

The focus of the discussion is also crucial for the debriefing – we concentrate on the demonstrated skills, resources, generated ideas and "aha-moments" of the participants. This means that the debrief, or solution, comes from the participants themselves. Just like in individual solution-focused coaching, where you only know which question you asked when you hear the answer of your client, you also can only say after an activity what it was good for. For this reason it makes sense to start the debrief with very open questions like: "What did you notice?" or "What did you discover during the activity?" We do our best to

> *We concentrate on the demonstrated or discovered skills, the resources that generated ideas and "Aha-moments" of the participants.*

choose activities that can create a specific effect or ask questions which direct our clients' focus in a specific direction, but it is really our participants who have to tell us which progress they were able to make in an activity.

In the second step we pose appreciative questions about the resources which were discovered in the exercise: "Who contributed to the solution?", "What did they contribute?", "What do the activities say about our strengths and resources?", "What would you like to keep doing in daily life?"

Since we do not assume that the context of an exercise and the context of daily life are the same, it is necessary to plan a transfer of learning from activities into daily life. This can be facilitated by asking about where the resources that were discovered already show up in daily business: "Where have you noticed something similar in your daily life?" or by asking about how what was learned can be transferred to a different context. You can also work with scaling question: "Where were you on a scale of 1 to 10 regarding topic xyz during the activity?", "Which number would you give yourself in your daily business life?", "What is already working well in daily life?", "How would you notice that you reached one step higher on the scale?"

## Summary

Good Working Relationship
- Glues Clues
- One for all and all for one
- A personal superlative

Pre-session Change
- Collecting of participants' comments on "What is better in your view?" on a flipchart
- Small group discussions about: "What is better?"
- Speed dating: "What is better?"
- Individual work with Post-It notes: "What is better?"
- Work in small groups or pairs on: "What did we get right in the last months?"

Goal setting
- Plenary discussion with flipchart
- Pretended feedback round
- Letter from the future
- Drawing a picture

Coping-Questions
- Plenary discussion
- Work in pairs or small groups

Scaling questions
- Scaling Walk
- Plenary discussion with flipchart
- Raising your hand
- Humming

## Exceptions and resources

Miracle question
- Facilitation techniques
- Small groups or plenary
- Miracle board
- Role-play in the future / videos
- Pin board-timeline
- A fictitious meeting
- Going for a walk

Small steps
- Decision making
- Prioritizing

Confidence, benefit and appreciative feedback
- Confidence scale
- Confidence snowball fight
- Positive Paranoia
- Resource gossip of the consultants
- Atmosphere / benefit diagram

Reflecting Team
Tetralemma
Turning other team coaching exercises into solution-focused exercises

# Team coaching processes

## A simple process

"Every case is different" is an important basic tenet of solution-focused consulting. Defining standard processes is therefore a bit counter-intuitive. Our suggestions for processes are best understood as ideas and inspirations. It is like when you are in a big outdoor shop

*Every case is different!*

trying to gear up for your expedition. You think about where you will be going and check out the wares with that in mind. You know what you will probably need but you also are inspired by the offer.

As already mentioned above, the process which we use most often is structured like this.

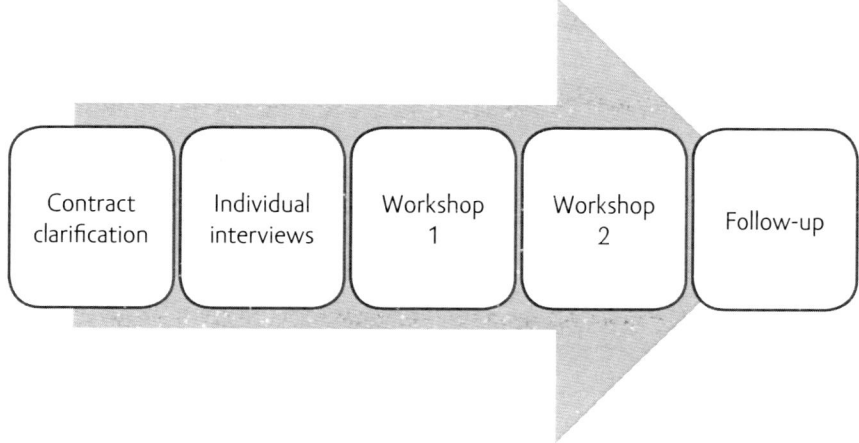

| Contract clarification | Individual interviews | Workshop 1 | Workshop 2 | Follow-up |

## Contract clarification

*General remarks*

To clarify a contract or a proposal for work in team coaching, it is quite possible to use the same questions as the ones used for goal negotiation.

Here is a short summary of what is relevant before entering into a team coaching process:

At the beginning, it is most important to find out from the sponsors of the team coaching what should be different after the team coaching process than before. Oftentimes, people and organizations do not have a clear picture of what would be an ideal or better state. Sometimes this ideal or better state can only be elicited by working with the team members. As already mentioned in our example on the useless presentation coaching, it is important not to fall into the "language trap" and believe you know what the sponsor or team means when they are using a general term. For example, if you are asked to "increase motivation," you do not really know as a consultant what should be better afterwards – you have to ask. It is best if you can get the sponsor or team leader to describe in detail what that change will be and which context it can be measured in or will be noticed.

Some team coaching processes last for months and you cannot assume that you can "clarify" the process and the contract once and for all at the beginning of the process. With longer processes it makes sense to plan "update conversations" or "fine tune meetings" right from the beginning. No plan survives the clash with reality.

## The grammar of the team: language and style

When sponsors choose a team coach they often ask about relevant experience in the sector or industry of the company. The assumption is that it is useful if the team coach has already worked together with people from similar professions. For solution-focused consulting such experience is not as important. For us, knowing about a similar problem or

*No plan survives the clash with reality.*

a similar group has two sides: on the one hand, it is useful to know a little bit about the language of the team members and what they might mean. On the other hand, it is always dangerous to assume you know what somebody means and therefore stop asking questions.

Knowing the language and the working style of clients can be useful for the "standing" of the consultants. You can ask yourself why it is necessary for consultants to give a good impression and to demonstrate standing. Actually, what is in focus here is the confidence of the team members. The consultant who does not fulfill any of the competence markers of the team will not be taken seriously by the team members. They will have a difficult time thinking seriously about the questions of the consultant. Knowing about the team's competence markers is therefore interesting: is it a certain presence, a certain language or outfit, or something entirely different? The consultant can then choose to fulfill these competence markers within the limits of his or her own possibilities to feel credible.

## Context – what do I need to know?

In contrast to systemic consultancy, solution-focused consultants do not assume that it is necessary to collect information about the system before the start of the consulting work. Solution- focused consulting aims at useful interactions between the consultant with active people and it always happens in "person grammar." The language is about who does what and how, and who would like to change what they do or the way they do things. It is about concrete actions and thoughts of people. The consultant does not assume an observer stance and does not think that information about structures can be separated from the people within these structures. Learning about how the organization functions, the organizational structures and ways of decision-making are only important in so far as it helps the consultant interact with the people in the organization.

Therefore, this is also not important for the solution-focused consultant to become aware of his or her own "inner picture" or ideas about organization. Reflecting one's previous experiences with systems like family or school is often an important part of systemic consulting training. The goal here is to ensure the consultant remains independent from possible unconscious assumptions about how systems function. Since these are irrelevant for solution-focused consulting, it is not necessary to delve into these issues in trainings for solution-focused consulting. This is why our trainings are usually shorter. The devil is again in the detail – it sounds simple, but it is not easy. As solution-focused consultants, we know that our own assumptions and ideas are not relevant for the consulting process. But how do you manage to let go of your own assumptions and how do you create an "assumption free" conversation with clients? For beginners in the solution-focused approach, it is useful to start by pretending not to have assumptions. You notice your own assumptions as they arise, let them go, and return your focus to the client by asking questions about goals, the miracle, resources, and exceptions or small steps. But back to the contract negotiation in which working without assumptions is so important.

Steve de Shazer often started solution-focused interviews by asking, "So what do you do with yourself the whole day?" which is a very relaxed question about the daily life of his clients. The answer to this question provides clues about the resources of the client and an overview of the context in which the client would like an improvement to take place. For the same reason, we want to find out a little bit about what everybody does the whole day before starting the solution-focused team coaching. We ask the following questions (which incidentally are not so different from those that would be asked in systemic coaching; the difference is mainly the philosophical background and the kinds of information that is picked up from the answer):

- Who is part of the team?
- What are the people like? (age, education, general mood, competence markers)
- What is going well and what would they like to keep doing?
- Who should participate in the team coaching? (This question can also be asked later.)
- What is the team doing the whole day?
- What is the main task of the team within the organization?
- What is the company strategy, mission, and vision? What is important for the company?
- What does the team have to get right next year?
- What are the interfaces of the team? (The answer to this question is very useful for ensuing questions about who would notice a change.)

It is also important to find out a little bit about the decision-making limits of the team. It can be very frustrating if the team identifies useful steps in the team coaching process, and then it turns out they cannot be carried out. Naturally, the team knows whether things that have been decided on in the team coaching sessions can be implemented by the team members and lie within their responsibilities. We usually confirm this when we are asking about what the next steps are when we are creating action lists. It can be very helpful to talk to the Human Resource department or the team leader about the decision-making limits regarding what can or cannot be changed by the team before entering into a team coaching process.

## Different origins of the request
### Request by HR

We are most often approached for team coaching by the Human Resource department. The HR department has usually been notified by someone in the company who indicated that there is room for improvement in the team. Either the team has approached the HR department, the team leader is asking for help, or it might even be one of the team leader's superiors who sees that something might be changed for the better.

When the coach is approached by HR, you are not speaking directly to the client in the first step. HR usually talks to several consultants about the issue at hand before recommending a team coach. HR has been told about the issues and tasks of the team and usually knows what should be improved.

Therefore, in the clarification phase with HR, you are usually dealing with two issues: On the one hand, it is important to find out as much as possible about the goals of the team coaching and have the request for proposal as clear as possible in order to be able to decide whether this is a contract the team coach can and would like to enter into. On the other hand, the conversation with HR is also a form of a "sales pitch" in which the consultant would like to convince the organization that he or she is the right partner for these kinds of jobs. In our experience it is important to focus on the fit between company and consultants. If an organization has clear ideas of what should happen in the team coaching, and these clear ideas do not fit with a solution-focused approach, it is most often better not to put in a proposal.

*Example 12:* **But where is your feedback?**

> *We had been asked by an internationally operating bank to conduct a simple team coaching process for them. The team had been working together since three years. Half a year ago they had a change in the team leadership and were now working with the new team leader. Collaboration was working very well and the team wanted to take some time out to make sure to be able to continue this good beginning. We thought that this fit very well with the solution-focused approach: We would scale with the team where they are on the scale of 1 to 10, 10 being optimal collaboration (whatever this means for the team) and take it from there.*
>
> *HR had asked to be able to join in. The lady in question was a young, motivated and very friendly member of the training and development department. We thought that she could help with her perspective and observational resources, and generally be very useful to have in the team coaching process since the team also trusted and respected her, so she attended the team coaching days.*
>
> *The team had wanted to talk about what was going well and what could even be a little bit better. They had also said that they would like to have some fun together and had said that they really appreciated interesting team exercises. Such kinds of exercises are easily integrated in solution-focused team coaching if you follow them up with a conversation about the strengths and resources of the team that appeared in the exercise. You can then talk about where these strengths and resources are visible in the daily life of the team. If the team cannot spot the same strengths in daily life, you can talk about how the exercise made it possible for the team to demonstrate their strengths and how they could show up in daily life, too.*
>
> *In this case we carried out a rather traditional team exercise: building*

*a bridge. The team got the task to build a bridge which would hold two water bottles using the facilitation materials available. The team was very successful and creative in their solution-finding approach. In the debriefing phase of the exercise, the team members realized that they were able to integrate and build on different ideas very well. They also appreciated the careful team leadership by their boss. They also realized a few other strengths that had become visible. The team was able to plan how they would use these strengths in their daily lives and everybody left with the feeling that this had been a very useful exercise and a meaningful conversation.*

*You can imagine our surprise in the debriefing discussion with the training and development specialist when she said she was very disappointed in how this exercise had been conducted. She knew this exercise from other workshops. Her expectation was that we, as team coaches, would observe the team in the solution-finding approach with detailed observation sheets or questionnaires (like in an assessment center) and then give every team member feedback on their team roles, their communication style, etc. She expected us to give each team member advice on how to improve his or her collaboration skills. In solution-focused consulting, we assume that every situation is different; therefore we cannot really draw conclusions which are valid for daily life in the team from the behavior of the team in an exercise like bridge building. The exercise only shows which kind positive behavior is possible for the team. Transferring these positive behaviors into daily life requires deliberation and planning. For us, such an exercise is more an occasion for constructive conversation similar to a question about team resources or exceptions then a diagnostic tool.*

*Only in the debriefing with the training and development specialist did we notice what we should have clarified beforehand: What were her expectations about the debriefing and use of experiential exercises?*

*ROI of the work of the Human Resource department is often difficult to measure or quantify – therefore the HR department is also happy when they can demonstrate the result of their work in concrete numbers.*

> *Which methodologies in team coaching does she know and what has she experienced as useful?*

Apart from questions about the context as they are listed above, the following questions to the HR department would have proven useful:

- Which kind of team coaching processes have you observed in the last few months?
- What was important for you?
- What is important for you about this coaching process?
- What is important for you in the collaboration with external consultants? What were some of the most positive experiences with external consultants?
- Have you been trained as a coach? Which training did you attend? What did you like about it?
- What would you like to know about us?
- What tells you that we could be the right consultants for this project?

Other interesting questions could be:

- What are some of the instruments for HR management that the company uses?
- What are your company "values"? Are there competency frameworks, leadership guidelines or other important instruments that you use?
- Are there regular surveys for example employee opinion surveys?

The answers to these questions can help us understand a bit about the context in which an improvement for the team needs to fit. For example, it would not be very helpful if the team decided to do something which is in stark contrast to the company guidelines. If you as a consultant are interested in the instruments HR uses, you show respect and appreciation for the work of the Human Resource department. If there are regular employee opinion surveys, you might be able to "measure" the effect of the team coaching and how the team rates their collaboration in these surveys. The results of the work of consultants and coaches is often very difficult to measure, just like the work of the HR department in general. Oftentimes, the HR department is happy to be able to show how measures that they initiated affect employee opinion or even better, the bottom line. This way you can also demonstrate to the top management that your work has had a good return on their investment.

The HR department naturally also has an idea or an image of the team that you want to coach. The team members or the team leader have talked about their needs with the HR department. It is therefore useful to talk to HR about the exact goals that should be pursued in the team coaching. Of course, this does not replace talking to the team and the team leaders about what should be different after the team coaching. Questions for the HR department which relate to the goal could be:

- Suppose this team coaching is very useful for the team and the company who would notice?
- How would these individual stakeholders notice the improvement?
- What would be different for the team?
- How confident are you that the team can reach their goals?
- What makes you confident?
- What do you appreciate about this team?
- What do you appreciate about the team leader?

It is always helpful if you can partner with the HR department and ask about their experiences with coaching processes with the team in question to make sure that the methodology you are using in the team coaching fits the team. Here you could ask:

- What kind of coaching or training sessions has the team had in the past?
- What did they like? What did the team find less useful?

- What is the general approach of the team to measures like team coaching? Are they looking forward to it? Are they a little bit more skeptical?
- What is the atmosphere in the team like?

If you are able to partner with the HR department, you create the best conditions for the success of team coaching. In our experience it is much easier to design any type of coaching if you have a supportive HR department covering your back. This way, if there are any difficulties, you can start looking for a good solution together. Mutual appreciation prevents finger-pointing in difficult situations. Instead you can but to think about how you can continue in a way that benefits everybody. Nothing is more frustrating than when the HR department is blaming the consultants, the consultants are blaming the HR department, etc. when something is not working. Partnering in coaching and training makes much more sense for both sides. The good thing is that as solution-focused consultants we have the necessary know-how to build on our good relationship with the HR department.

## Request by the team leader

Direct requests for team coaching by the team leader are rare. Most often the conversation with the team leader or team members is the second step after clarifying the contract, respectively the sales meeting with the HR department. It is absolutely mandatory for the success of the team coaching to talk to the team leader before you start. Here you can also ask a few questions about the context. What is most important is to find out about the goal of the team leader and the methodology the team is comfortable with. Questions about the context are the same as those listed above. Here are a few more possible questions:

- Suppose the team coaching process is very useful for you and your team. Who would notice a change? What would they notice?
- Which of these changes would be especially desirable or important for you?
- On a scale of 1 to 10, where 10 is that you have already reached

these individual goals and one means that you are just starting to think about them, where is the team in your view? (Here you can use one or several scales depending on the goals of the team.)

- What do you notice about the team that tells you that you are already at an X and not at one?
- Who would notice X+1? What would that tell them?
- What should stay the same in your team?
- What do you appreciate about your team?
- What makes you confident that these improvements can be achieved?

We often jot down the answers to these questions on a piece of paper. It can be quite practical to conduct such conversations on the telephone – this way you can type away while you are talking and you have a good overview of the starting point of the process. The results can also be made available to the team before the team coaching.

### Interviews

After clarifying the contract with the Human Resource department and the team leader, we often ask to carry out short interviews with the team members. These interviews provide the possibility to get to know each other and also offer the opportunity for a more exact goal setting process. These interviews are solution-focused interviews – so they often increase the confidence of the team members that something can change for the better. It is also sometimes useful to ask other stakeholders, customers or other interface points of the team similar questions.

Example 13: **A second chance**

A high-tech company had conducted the standardized employee opinion survey: "A great place to work." They had found out there were significant deviations in one German team in contrast to other international teams. They did not seem happy with their leadership *at all and there were other topics which popped up in the survey which made it seem useful to conduct a team coaching process.*

*In the interviews I asked the team members about their general assessment of the team situation first: "On a scale of 1 to 10, where ten means that you come to work every morning happy and willing to give your best and one is the opposite, where are you now?" Many were around 7. When I then asked: "What tells you that you are already on a seven and not on a one?" I found out they thought their work was very interesting and provided a great technological challenge. Team cohesion and the atmosphere within the team were very good. However, before I could get in the next question, many team members told me that everything else – and especially their boss – was a catastrophe.*

*One team member especially had taken on something like an inofficial leadership role and was very upset about his boss: "He is a complete loser! Our meetings are completely chaotic. Whenever he has to defend our interests internationally, he simply gives in and we end up with only those tasks that are too difficult for everybody else. He also does not ask about the general strategy or takes care that we get the resources we need. I would be much better at this! He never gives us feedback and we feel completely left out in the cold."*

*I was surprised by how strongly he felt. I would not have expected this from this rather rational and dry engineer. So I mumbled something along the lines of: "That sounds terrible – I am impressed that you still like your work that much, anyway." When I had recovered from the shock, I tried a confidence scale: "On a scale of 1 to 10, where 10 means that you are extremely confident that something can change with regard to this topic and one is the opposite, where are you now?" The engineer looked at me very surprised. He started thinking and there was a relatively long, not extremely comfortable silence. He finally said: "So you mean that for this thing to be successful at all, I really need to give my boss a second chance?" I could see in his eyes that he was also seeing the humorous element of the situation. So I threw my hands up in the air and said: "Meeee? I'm not thinking anything – you just said this!" We both laughed and continued with a very construc- tive conversation.*

*This little episode shows that the interviews are not mainly for data collection. They prepare the ground for a successful beginning of the team coaching.*

The questions for the interviews naturally depend on the task or the re- quest. The main difference is what you take as a 10 on the scale. Here are some sample questions:

- What is your role in the team? What is your task? What would you do the whole day?
- On a scale of 1 to 10, where 10 means
  - that you go to work in the morning happy and in a good mood willing to do your best
  - that your team problem has been solved
  - that you work well together
  - ... with one for the opposite / the beginning / the most dif- ficult moment, etc., where do you see the team now?
- What tells you the team is on X and not on 1? What else?
- Who contributes what to that? What else?
- Who would notice an improvement to X+1? What would they notice what that would tell them?
- What are some of things that we should definitely talk about in the team coaching?
- What do you appreciate about your team?
- What is your experience with team coaching workshops?
- Which methods have you already used that you found useful?

The team interviews most often happen on the telephone so that you can type while talking. Our experience is that the relative anonymity of the telephone call sometimes even makes it easier for people to confide in you and to speak about what they really want to see happening after a team coaching process. After every interview we read our notes to the interview partners to make sure that we did not misunderstand them. The interviews take around 15 minutes, so that for a team of eight people you have an interview time of approximately 2 hours.

## Report

The interviews result in a report which is sent to all team members and the team leader. In this report we summarize what the team members and the team leader said and (re)formulate what we heard in a solution-focused way. When we are doing interviews, in contrast to asking about coaching goals via an online survey, we have the opportunity to ask what people would like to happen instead of their complaints. In the report we state the problems that were mentioned – solution-focused does not mean problem-phobic. However, instead of focusing on what is going wrong at the moment, we use statements describing who would like to work on what with which goal in mind or about what the situation would look like if the problems were solved. Instead of writing: "Our planning process is chaotic. Our projects always run over time and budget. And to make matters worse, we start arguing and blaming each other when that happens."

We phrase it like this: "The majority of the team would like to have a well-planned and orderly project management process. When problems appear people should jointly look for solutions. A peaceful and constructive process would be something everybody would appreciate."

The topics that are mentioned most often are usually those that have a very high priority in the team coaching. If all team members mentioned in the interviews that they would like to work on better information sharing, the report will state this in the beginning and it will probably be talked about in the workshop. Topics that only a few team members mention are also integrated into the report, but usually worked upon later in the team coaching process. Sometimes the situation has improved enough after the most important problems have been solved that the team can solve the other issues without the consultant.

The solution-focused report mentions:

- positively stated goals that can be described in observable behavior and are within the influence of the team
- exceptions, resources and strengths of the team which make the team confident that they can reach their goals
- sometimes feedback from the consultant about what he or she is impressed with about the team.

You could say that the report has a similar function as the feedback of the therapist after a session of solution-focused therapy. The report is written in the language of the clients and should meet with their approval. This strengthens the focus on the positive: the confidence that steps in the direction of this goal can be made. At the same time the report strengthens the perception of the team members for their respective appreciation of each other and thereby the cohesion and positive work atmosphere in the team.

*Example 14:* **An anonymized report**

*What do you have to get right in the next future?*

*Most team members mentioned the end of the fiscal year and the tax and management reports which they have to get right. In their view they are quite stressful and a lot of work. It is very important for everybody to ensure a peaceful, professional and appreciative work atmosphere during that time, so that this difficult time does not become more difficult through personal disagreements.*

*Some mentioned that they would also like to continue to improve the relationship with Hungary to optimize own processes.*

*Solution-focused does not mean problem-phobic.*

*Dealing with the uncertainty of the future development of the department was mentioned as a difficulty by many team members. They said that the highest possible transparency* about the planned steps in the direction of changing the team structure or further outplacement would be very useful. There were concerns that the team would not be able to fulfill their task and that the amount of work would be too much if the team was made smaller. Some team members were worried that their own job might be in danger due to further outplacement. Even the team members who mentioned these concerns understand the economic situation of the company. If changes are necessary, they will be understood. The team member really appreciate transparency to be able to react quickly and to know that they do not have to worry unnecessarily.

On a scale of 0 to 10, where 10 is that you like going to work in the morning to be able to do a good job together with the rest of the team and one is the opposite, where are you now?
1; 2-3; 0; 2-3; 5-6; 2; under 5; 8; 9; over 5

What is going well?
All said that they were happy to be able to get the work done at a high quality level. When they are able to communicate unemotionally and in a neutral way, daily collaboration works well. People can rely on each other in the daily operations. Most team members said that they like the work itself. It is interesting, varied, and challenging in a good way. All team members feel committed to their work and also, for example, work from home even when they are not feeling well. Attempts to structure the work by a weekly plan have worked partially.

Collaboration in small groups works well. Everybody has at least one person that they get along with well and where the collaboration is seamless and trusting. Professional collaboration works well. Team members help each other, but can also replace each other if necessary, and people trust that the work gets done.

The team leader is highly valued due to her skills and in-depth knowledge of the subject matter. Some also mentioned they appreciate that she takes care of her team members, for example, by making sure that *the weeks around Christmas are not filled with additional projects and people can take time off. Some team members appreciate her direct and open communication style.*

## What would a small step forward look like?

*Almost all team members mentioned that the trust in other team members had clearly suffered through the recent incidents. It is important to experience again that it is possible to interact honestly and trusting without having the feeling that this will result in negative consequences elsewhere. Overall, all team members would like to return to a more respectful way of interacting.*

*Almost all team members said that currently there were many misunderstandings along with different and more-or-less distrustful interpretations of the behavior of the other team members. A first step forward was described as follows: Instead of guessing what someone means by a certain behavior and interpreting it as an insult or offense, it would be better to approach the person in question in a friendly or neutral way and ask for an explanation. The other person should then react in an equally friendly or neutral way and, in turn, their explanation would be believed by the asker. The advantage would be that this openness would result in more confidence in team communication. People would stop carrying chips on their shoulders and would return to communicating more spontaneously since they would not have to reflect on how something they say will be interpreted. Through the feedback on what is meant by what is said, team members could also learn about the impact of their behavior on others. Team members who are more dominant and direct could learn to utilize this in a useful way for the team, and the quieter team members could learn to speak up more often.*

*Many team members would like to experience the team as a whole and less as a collection of cliques. The communication in the whole team could be improved. The team members would take care to talk positively about each other and also about members of other departments in their absence.*

*Many team members wanted a more constructive way of dealing with mistakes. Team and leadership could think about how they could deal with mistakes in a way that makes it possible for the person who made the mistake to learn from it and avoid it in the future. Many think that appreciation is the key. Criticism should be voiced in a helpful and appreciative fashion, and the people whose behavior is being criticized might take care to see it as an attempt to help. If something happens that somebody does not like, he or she should talk directly to the person in question and clarify the issue before someone else finds out about it.*

*Some team members said that there were still opportunities to improve work allocation and substitution plans. It would be good to think about ways in which this process could run more smoothly. One way of improving the situation immediately would be if team members could ask each other for help without fear of losing face.*

*Most team members expect from the team leadership that they keep an eye on the content side of the work and that they also recognize current conflicts in the team, listen to all sides constructively, and help work toward a solution. For some team members it would be important to know that all team members are being treated fairly and equally and that their competencies are measured according to the same criteria. Some would like more clarity and transparency about their own development with regard to the goals of the team. A few team members would like more careful communication. Clarity about the future of the team was mentioned as important by some.*

*The team miracle: Suppose a miracle happens and all problems in the team are solved "just like this" – how would you begin to notice?*

*Many team members had a hard time imagining a miracle that would include all members of the existing team – however, after some thoughts, it became clear that the miracle looks very similar for all team members.*

*The team members would notice a miracle immediately when they* come to work and are greeted in a friendly and relaxed way in the morning. They would have fun in their work, would laugh together and you could see people standing between cubicles talking, being interested in each other and appreciating each other's company. The atmosphere would be open and you would sometimes hear: "Oh, I'm sorry I made a stupid mistake; I'm sorry – could you help me resolve it?" The reply would be an understanding offer of help. If somebody realizes that a mistake has been made, he or she would say something like: "I noticed this … could you explain? I think something might have gone wrong there." Then people would set out to look for a solution in a calm and neutral tone. You would hear team members talk positively about the team and other team members. They would also praise each other. When somebody needs to continue working on a task that somebody else began, the information meetings would be respectful, complete and polite.

Some said that after the miracle there would be something like a daily meeting to set goals. This could happen in the middle of the morning when everybody had a chance to get an overview of what needs to get done during the day. The work of the team would be everybody's responsibility. Conflicts would be clarified in the team. Processes would run more smoothly.

**On a scale of 0 to 10 how confident are you that you can make progress in the direction of this miracle?**
*5; 5; 5-6; 3; 3-4; 1; 0; 2; a little*

**What gives you a little confidence?**
*Many team members said that they were concerned that due to the previous conflicts and hurt feelings it might not be possible to regain a trustful and positive work atmosphere. To be more confident they would have to see an effort to realize that there are first steps to positive changes. Along with their positive changes, it will also be necessary to take them at face value and assume that the other person is*

*doing their best to alleviate the situation. This is the only way that trust can be re-created on a long-term basis.*

*The team members also agree that team problems should only be talked about in the team for a certain period of time. What also makes the team members confident is that they value the high professionalism of every team member – even among the team members who personally do not like each other.*

*Since the time when it was worst, the team behavior has already become a little bit better. Some see there is the desire to change something and hope that by creating and abiding by communication rules, there can at least be a step in the direction of positive, professional relationships.*

## Workshop

After interviewing team members and sending out the report, the goals and issues for the team workshop are usually clear. We have never experienced a team who was not clear about who could not agree, on the most part, about topics which needed to be discussed. A lot of the goal setting happens before the workshop. This is why the workshop itself can be relatively short. In the most cases a workshop of 6 to 8 hours is sufficient. Sometimes you also only need half a day. The structure of the workshop follows the topics that have been identified by the team. Please find possibilities for restructuring and facilitating such workshops in the chapter on tools.

## Follow-up

Solution-focused consulting assumes that a lot of the desired changes happen in the daily life of the team, not necessarily during the consultation or coaching. It is therefore useful to call in a follow-up session a short while after the first workshop. Just like in a solution-focused individual coaching, we then ask the team what is better. The beauty of the team coaching situation is that you can ask who contributed to each reported change and who made the improvement possible.

In especially difficult or critical cases we sometimes insert another round of interviews before the follow-up session to find out confidentially if something has improved in the perception of the individual team members. It is important to make sure that the question "what is better" is not interpreted as if answers about what stayed the same or what still needs to be better are not allowed. This question gives the team members the opportunity to think about what has improved – it is not about pretending or putting a brave face on the matter.

Further points on the agenda of the follow-up meeting are all the topics that have not yet been talked about, have appeared in the meantime, or items that are still not at a state where the team wants them to be. These topics are discussed in the same way as before by scaling, in small groups or the plenary. The main focus is planning first steps in the direction of an improvement.

Theoretically there could be more sessions until all topics have been talked about. In our experience teams are usually happy with two sessions. After these sessions, the team most often has enough confidence in their own ability to solve problems so that no more external facilitation is necessary. In the follow-up session, we also always ask the team what was useful for a positive change and what they would like to continue doing – which also strengthens their ability to find solutions by themselves. Sometimes we also ask about what the team will do if the situation gets worse unexpectedly or if there are setbacks so they are prepared and know what to do. Such consulting strategies might be bad for our business, but they are very helpful for the self-confidence of the team.

## Other processes

Obviously, we did not invent solution-focused team coaching. There are a few other models which have been deployed successfully internationally.

Ben Furman and Tapani Ahola developed the concept called "Twin Star." In this concept, they collate their experience and learning about how to create happiness at the workplace. Under the label "reteaming," they offer a solution- focused process for teams or groups. In the meantime, this offer for organizations has been renamed "Co-operation." Their books on "Twin

Star," "Reteaming" and "Co-operation" are available through Ben Furman's website: www.benfurman.com.

Daniel Meier designed another solution-focused method for team development. We were so enthusiastic about his book, "Team Coaching with the SolutionCircle," that we translated it from its German original into English, together with Jenny Clarke of Solutionbooks. You can find this book and many practical tips and hints, along with agendas and frameworks for entire workshops.

In the following sections, we would like to provide an overview of other existing methods.

## SolutionCircle

The SolutionCircle transfers the philosophy of solution-focused individual coaching to team development. Each SolutionCircle can have the following steps (naturally, always adapted to the issue at hand):

1. Preparing the ground
2. Expectations and goals
3. Hot topics
4. Highlights
5. Future perfect
6. Scaling dance
7. Steps
8. Personal mission

## Preparing the ground

For Daniel Meier, "Preparing the Ground" is the initial phase of team coaching together with the group. This step serves to create trust between the team members. The team coach creates an atmosphere conducive to working together in general. The coach tells the group what has already happened before the workshop, for example, clarification of the contract or whatever else he or she has learned about the team. The team coach takes care to mention any resources of the team that he or she has heard about. He or she also talks about the decision framework of the workshop: what can be changed and what cannot be changed. Then the coach quickly describes the solution-focused method of working: the topic is finding solutions to the team problems and not analyzing problems or delving deeply into the past. The role of the coach as facilitator who is responsible for the process (and not the content) is clarified.

Daniel Meier also recommends creating a flipchart with "housekeeping rules" for the workshop. This step is often used in workshop situations. Unfortunately, it is hardly ever talked about what happens once somebody breaks them. You cannot control what happens during the workshop, and you as facilitator have to deal with what happens moment-for-moment during the process. By following the mood of the team, you can also skip the step of agreeing to workshop rules, in our view.

## Expectations and goals

The coach and the team agree on which goals should be reached during the workshop. It is also important for Daniel Meier to clarify the criteria that tell the team that their engagement in the workshop was worth the effort. This step is facilitated as a plenary discussion or in small groups using similar questions like the ones we noted above. Daniel Meier discusses very usefully how the team coach deals with the answers of the participants to goal-oriented questions. Often goals are formulated in a negative way or are very vague. The team coach helps the team to formulate positive, realistic and concrete goals.

## Hot topics

"Solution-focused doesn't mean problem phobic" – you often hear this sentence from solution- focused practitioners. Daniel Meier picks up on this basic attitude in his step named "hot topics." Participants are asked to write the most important problems on index cards. These are then clustered and prioritized. Afterwards small groups of people interested in this specific problem work on possible solutions.

## Highlights

After working on the hot topics, the facilitation of the SolutionCircle returns to examining the positive experiences of the team. The team collects positive experiences, sparkling moments, and highlights of the last few weeks in small groups or in the plenary. Afterwards they analyze how these highlights or sparkling moments became possible, who contributed and which strengths of the team became apparent in these moments.

## Future perfect

In the step "future perfect", the groups that formed according to their interests in the step "hot topics" work on a rich, positive description of their desired future regarding the respective topic. The focus is on what the world will look like when the problem is gone – on solution-building rather than problem-solving.

## Scaling dance

Helpful differences are identified using a physical scale in the room. Team members position themselves wherever they think the team is at. They then turn their attention to what tells them that they are no longer at zero. In the next step the team physically takes one step in the direction of 10 and then talks about how they would notice that they have moved one step ahead. This usually automatically leads to developing small steps.

## Steps

This step serves to formulate concrete actions. Daniel Meier recommends that the team not only write down what to do, but also which resources they have that they might use in their further development. These resources can be people, processes, funds, in short everything that might help. The team is also invited to think about how they can keep the process that they have started running.

## Personal mission

The attention of each team member is focused on small signs of progress by having each team member go on a personal mission. Team members select their own activities to support the team process. These activities, however, are not made public. One team member might decide to speak up more often in team meetings while the other team member might make sure that the documentation is in order every Friday. The personal activity can also be an observation task: each team member collects the signs of improvement they perceive over the next week. Collecting these signs of improvement can also be a very nice start for the follow-up workshop.

### Reteaming

Ben Furman's and Tapani Ahola's "Reteaming" is a structured process which can be used by individuals to make progress on an issue. It can also be used for team or organizational development. Over the years, there have been several versions of the re-teaming process. The steps are quite logical, however, there is some leeway in the order in which each step is taken. Here are the steps:

### Describe your dream

In the first step you describe in detail what a desired future will look like. You visualize – just like in the miracle question – a situation in which this future is already happening. It is important to talk about what will be better or different in detail. This dream is the basis for the re-teaming process.

### Identify a goal

The dream is now broken down into smaller goals which need to be achieved in order for the dream to become reality. In the further process, one goal is selected

### Engage supporters

The team or the individual going through the re-teaming process creates a list of all people who could be helpful in the quest to achieve the goal. These are then approached and informed about the goal. They are also asked for their support.

## Describe the benefits achieving your goal will have

People think about what exactly will be better once the goal has been reached. If, for example, the goal is "better communication," you ask exactly how the individual or the team will notice that communication has improved and what has become better or more possible through better communication.

## Recognize which progress has already taken place

You usually do not start at zero. In this step, you think about what has already happened with regard to the goal. In the case of "better communication," for example, the team would write down all the signs of communication that is already happening in the way that they would like.

## Visualize the progress to come

The team or individuals think about the steps which are necessary to reach the goal. (In our opinion, this is slightly alien to solution-focused philosophy since we generally assume that you cannot plan all steps from 0 to 10 because the world will look different after each step. However, this planning process is very compatible to the language and world of business.) This step can be facilitated well by using a timeline into the future on a long flipchart.

## Acknowledging that it will not be easy

As in classic project management, the team or individual thinks about the possible obstacles and why it might be difficult for them to reach their goal. Who or what could work against the desired solutions and what does the team or individual anticipate? For example, if the goal is "improving communication," a difficulty might be that there is not enough time for an exchange.

## Identify reasons for optimism

In this step, you think about how you will overcome the obstacles. You will also identify the reasons you are confident that you will reach your goal in spite of the difficulties.

## Getting commitment

Every team member decides on the necessary steps they want to carry out and informs the others. This results in greater commitment and a moral obligation to actually follow through.

## Chart progress

The next meetings with the team or individual serve to follow up on these steps: What happened? What still needs to happen? What worked? Where do you have to make adjustments? This step is very close to traditional project management – very pragmatic and down to earth. The only (possible) difference is that people will try to adopt a non-blaming approach when something did not happen as planned.

## Dealing with setbacks

If something does not work as the team or individual planned, in other words when there are setbacks, we ask without assigning blame what we can do to mitigate. It is important not to give up hope that you can reach your goal. If all fails, it is still possible to identify new and more realistic goals.

## Celebrate success and thank the supporters

Once the goal is reached, a celebration is called for. In a business environment, this can be a simple "project review" in which you do not only reflect on what went well and what could have gone better, but also celebrate with coffee, cake, champagne, and appetizers. You can invite all the people who contributed to the success. The most important success factors are highlighted once more and thereby engrained for future projects.

Tapani Ahola and Ben Furman offer training programs over several days in which you can also gain a certification: http://www.cooperationtraining.com

### Twin Star

"The Twin Star book – a solution-focused approach to improving the psychosocial environment of the workplace –" by Tapani Ahola and Ben Furman, does what the title states. It introduces a concept for improving work atmosphere and employee satisfaction. The authors share our reservations with regard to the omnipresent surveys on employee satisfaction. Solution-focused practitioners assume that you can improve employee satisfaction without a prior measurement and anal-

*Solution-focused practitioners assume that you can improve the employee satisfaction without a prior measurement and analysis of the reasons of possible dissatisfaction.*

ysis of the reasons for possible dissatisfaction. "Twin Star" is a structured summary of the authors' learnings from many "reteaming"-processes. Ben Furman and Tapani Ahola distilled a few crucial factors leading to a positive working atmosphere and a willingness to cooperate on the side of the employees.

- Appreciation
- Fun (and a sense of humor)
- Success
- Caring

According to Ben Furman and Tapani Ahola, not only these positive factors are crucial. Another important factor is being able to deal with the main difficulties of daily business life:

- Problems (and the discussions about problems)
- Hurts (having hurt someone or having been hurt)
- Setbacks (and other failures)
- Criticism (criticizing someone and being criticized)

These eight factors are depicted as two stars, a positive and a negative one. This is also where the name "Twin Star" comes from.

## Appreciation

It is essential for a good working atmosphere that members of an organization show mutual respect and appreciation for each other's work. This is not achieved by simply shouting "great job," but by positive feedback that shows that others are interested in your work and that they appreciate how you do it. There are many ways of expressing appreciation: asking others for advice, being interested in the viewpoints of the other person, telling third parties about the good work others are doing. Of course, in order to get to a positive work atmosphere, team members also need to learn how to accept appreciative feedback from others. Ben Furman and Tapani Ahola recommend thanking others for the praise and then passing it on to those who have contributed to making it possible. Instead of simply saying: "Thank you" you would say: "Thank you! You know, my colleagues really helped me with this project – it would not have been possible without them." Another factor in creating a climate of appreciation is the permission to actively ask for positive feedback from the other team members. This way, you show that you care about their views of your work.

## Fun (and a sense of humor)

Fun and a sense of humor have definite health benefits for the workplace. Stress and exhaustion are reduced, and a sense of humor also leads to being able to face problems with more ease and optimism. If you have fun at your work, you become more creative. Even

*You enjoy coming to work more when you have the impression that your colleagues care about you as a person.*

if the work that needs to be done is monotone and boring, a team that has fun together can be the reason why people love coming to work in the morning. Of course, it is important that the team laughs together and that they do not laugh about each other.

## Success

Being proud or happy about your own achievements or the achievements of your team is one of the main factors for job satisfaction. This is why it makes sense to give every team member the opportunity to see and feel their achievements. You can do that by making small successes visible – such as talking about them and praising people. Everyone can contribute to everybody's job satisfaction by showing their happiness about the success that has been achieved. How you show your joy also makes a difference. If you include others in your success they will feel happy for you. So don't say: "I did it, I am great!" but "I did it, but I could only do that because we all worked together so well."

## Caring

People feel happier in their jobs when they feel appreciated as human beings and not only as an interchangeable cogwheel in a large machine. You enjoy coming to work more when you have the impression that your colleagues care about you as a person. Caring can be expressed in many different ways: showing empathy, asking about how others are doing, being interested in what the other person is working on, asking about things that you know the other person is interested in, etc. These small gestures should actually be almost second nature – did we not learn to be nice to each other in preschool? However, sadly enough, when we ask the miracle question in a team coaching session, the answer often is: "I would notice that a miracle happened when everybody greets me with a happy 'hello' in the morning."

## The "negative" star

Just like Ben Furman and Tapani Ahola we have also noticed that there are often situations in work environments that feel strange, uncomfortable, or that are even bothering people, but nobody dares to talk about it. In "Twin Star" you can find a down-to-earth script for dealing with these kinds of situations in a sensitive way:

- Ask the colleague for a conversation
- In the conversation, tell him or her that you are a little worried about him or her
- Listen well and show understanding and empathy
- Offer help but do not patronize by offering simple solutions
- Ask for a new conversation
- Follow up and, if necessary, offer further support (if necessary also by a professional)

This script is very helpful for people if they want to talk about things that seem uncomfortable or embarrassing.

Exercise 7: **Eau de collègue**

It is surprising how often the topic: "My colleague is a nice person, but he does have an unpleasant body odor... I really don't know how to mention it to him" comes up in leadership workshops or workshops on conflict management. Try to solve this situation with the help of the above script. You will see that it is quite useful to work with such a structure. Please turn the page only after you have jotted down a few thoughts yourself.

One possible solution
Asking the colleague for a conversation:

> "Hello Helga, I would like to talk to you about something – when would you have a few minutes? I would reserve the meeting room. Do not worry; it is nothing serious!"

In the conversation, tell him or her that you are a little worried about him or her:

> "Thank you for making time for our conversation. I do not want to beat around the bush. In the last weeks, I had conversations with two colleagues who noticed that you sometimes have an unpleasant body odor. Of course, this does not happen every day and it is really not a big thing. It is something that can happen to anybody. We all like you a lot and I wanted to speak to you about it directly. I thought that it would be better this way than if you found out about it through the grapevine – you know how such issues can develop..."

Listen well and show understanding and empathy

In most cases the person who you address with such an issue will feel a little bit embarrassed and will take care that this problem no longer occurs. It might also be that Helga had no idea that she had an unpleasant body odor and does not realize it when it happens. In this case you could:

Offer help but do not patronize by offering simple solutions

> "I do not know how I could help you with this – do you have an idea? What would be useful for you?"

Ask for a new conversation:
In this case, this will probably not be necessary. You might want to offer the following:

> "If you do not mind, could I let you know if I notice something when you are not aware that it is happening again?"

In the case of more difficult issues, for example alcoholism or the fact that someone often gets very upset and verbally abusive, you should agree on a second conversation later on if the colleague wants help. This is also true for the last possible step. Follow up and, if necessary, offer further support (if necessary also by a professional)

## Problems

We hope that after reading this book nobody will still think that it is useful to start looking for the root cause of a problem between people in order to solve it. Tapani Ahola and Ben Furman agree. However, this has not yet made the rounds in many teams and departments. Some-times it can be useful to teach teams about constructive ways of dealing with problems (of course, only if this is something that the team agrees would be useful). Tapani Ahola and Ben Furman also offer a structure for this.

1. "Convert the problems into goals
2. Make the goals interesting
3. Make the goals specific
4. Specify the steps to success
5. Make the goals viably achievable
6. Draw people's attention to progress
7. Give credit where it is due"
   (Ahola, T. & Furman, B., 2004: p. 68)

## Hurts

*Whenever people collaborate, there will be misunderstandings or the risk that people hurt each other.*

Whenever people collaborate, there will be misunderstandings or the risk that people hurt each other. This is simply a fact of life, and it makes no sense to put a lot of energy into trying to prevent misunderstandings and people hurting each other's feelings at all costs. However, it is still very important to look at and improve ways of dealing with misunderstandings or hurt feelings. Of course, the best solution is that the people involved talk about the issue quickly and face-to-face – sadly, it does not always happen this way. It really helps to develop a team culture in which an apology or a clarifying conversation is the normal way to react, when someone has accidentally hurt someone's feelings or when there was a misunderstanding that had undesirable consequences. Accepting these things as neither intentional nor completely unavoidable helps, too.

It often happens that third parties are being drawn into these kinds of situations. If these people understand how they can have a positive influence rather than fanning the fire, the team has acquired a very important asset. It is much better if third parties open an opportunity for the afflicted parties to talk to each other (rather than about each other) and clarify the issue and the emotions attached. When you have to deal with hurt feelings in a team coaching situation it often helps to not only talk about how we can alleviate and repair the feelings of hurt in the current situation, but also to talk about how people want to react if something like this happens again.

## Setbacks

A positive culture of dealing with mistakes and failures is very helpful for team cohesion, job satisfaction, and motivation. It makes a big difference whether every mistake that a colleague makes is seen as a confirmation of his or her incompetence, or if others understand that making mistakes is human and offer words of consolation and encouragement. We have met employees and managers in companies who seemed to be in constant upheaval about the mistakes and the stupidity of other people. You hear sentences like, "How stupid can you get!" or the famous sentence of some Hollywood directors, "I cannot WORK with people like that!" Just imagine how different the scene becomes when people react to a mistake by saying: "Oh well, things happen – I feel with you. Is there anything I can do to help repair this?" or "Shit! But you know, I really understand, this happened to me, too!" The most important step for advancing the team is to think about how you can avoid the mistake in the future.

## Criticism

"Constructive criticism" is an important topic in many team coaching sessions and workshops on leadership development. When a team wants some input on "how to do that," we often use components from "Twin Star." Our clients find the following five-step model very helpful. We found "taking critical feedback on board" in the book, but could not find "how to criticize constructively" in "Twin Star" – we must have learned it in one of Ben Furman's workshops and then continued to develop it further. We are sorry to say that we no longer know what is derived from Ben Furman's workshop and what we added or subtracted.

Taking critical feedback on bord::

1. Listen
2. Thank
3. Be accepting of the emotional reaction
4. Apologize for what happened
5. Turn the criticism into a hope that can be fulfilled.
   (Ahola & Furman, 2004, p.107)

Criticizing constructively:

1. Find a good moment
2. Give a concrete description of the problem
3. Describe what you want to happen instead
4. Agree on steps to take (on both sides)
5. Express confidence

Exercise 8: **Giving and taking criticism**

If you would like to exercise your skills in taking criticism on board and criticizing constructively, you could write a dialogue of a typical situation in which you would want to criticize someone or react positively to criticism. Many participants in our team coaching workshops had good experiences with these models.

## PET

The "Performance Enhancement Tool" was develop by Kirsten Dierolf and Christian Mühldorfer in 2008. It is a fast method for structuring change processes.

### Example 15

> Company Alpha has a problem. Alpha is a medium-sized supplier of plastic parts to the automotive industry with 250 highly specialized employees who are hard to get on the job market. Several of Alpha's customers have reduced their production on short notice and have cancelled orders they had previously submitted. This development was unforeseeable and surprised everybody at Alpha. The management is now in a tough spot and needs to develop a reaction: an action plan and also a plan for communicating the situation and the plan to the public. In such situations you typically have a few people who meet in a "war room" to create a plan. The result usually consists of very general statements which are scrutinized and opposed by those who were not involved in the decision-making process.

### Example 16

> Project managers at company Beta are suffering from the endless and futile discussions that arise in their long term projects around development of new pharmaceutical substances. In their opinion, two thirds of the meetings and workshops are too long, inefficient, and useless. On the one hand, they criticize that there is no buy-in to the results of these meetings. People tend to "tune out" when issues are being discussed that they are not directly concerned with. On the other hand, all agree that it is necessary to have an opportunity to agree on which process step follows the other and to have a streamlined and efficient way of operating. The next milestone makes another, hopefully more efficient, meeting necessary.

### Example 17

> Company Gamma is constructing a new production site. The project managers of the various contractors and architects, etc. have opposing

*views and many disagreements on how something should be done. There is little appreciation for the work and tasks assigned to each other. Discussions revolve around who is most dominant, who gives in, etc. The project manager of company Gamma said: "There are constant changes from all sides – we never really had the time to build a team or to agree on what needs to be done or how!"*

In the following discussion, we would like to describe in which way such situations contributed to our developing PET:

All these situations have in common that there is little time for making a decision. The people involved all have different information and individual, particular interests seem very important – sometimes even more important than the overall goal. As a consequence, a few people make decisions which then have to be "sold" to the other stakeholders. Depending on the communication savvy of the management or the decision-makers, this is more or less successful.

If you are interested in generating commitment, achieving a high involvement of all concerned, facilitating a buy-in, obtaining comprehensive information from all who are able to see more than their part of the story and are interested in the big picture, you often need a lot of time. Furthermore, if you would like to create action plans which are more than general statements of intent, this also requires a lot of time. You need meetings, large group interventions, a strategic change management plan, follow-ups, etc. In long-term projects, change projects or in agile software development, these methods (kick-offs, retrospectives, stand-up meetings, large group interventions) have become established as valuable tools for structuring change. However, when you are in a situation like one that is described above, time is crucial and, yet, you do not have any. PET is fast, saves time, and is still thorough enough to get everybody on board and develop lasting and substantial solutions.

One of the factors in PET which helps to gain commitment and a high buy-in is the fact that the result of every step is visualized and stays visible until the end of the process. The facilitator summarizes the results after each step and ensures that everybody agrees and is committed to continue work on the basis of what was just discussed.

Before starting a PET process, asking permission to engage in an unusual format of facilitation is useful. We clarify that there are only 3-15 minutes for each step and that this time is fixed: after 3-15 minutes we stop discussing the respective point. The participants are also assured that they will be able to gather and process all information in the minutes. The reduction in time also leads to a greater meeting discipline – pertinent contributions usually take precedence and are mentioned first. Usually there is not a lot of debate and discussion. Decisions are made faster by using facilitation methods like using sticky dots.

Since a PET workshop is a high-paced event using Post-It notes, rather than European style facilitation cards with pins and pin boards, is recommended. Additionally, it is quite useful to write down all the questions of the group and display them on a flipchart or as a heading on a pin- or whiteboard.

The timing of the seven steps is 1/4th for steps 1-3 and 3/4th of the time for steps 4-7. You need at least one hour – 2 hours with larger groups.

## Process

Step 1:     Goal Setting
- How will you notice that this workshop has been useful for you? (Write Post-it notes and collect them)

The participants are asked to cluster the individual contributions concerning goal settings immediately after writing them. After a short summary by the facilitator you continue with the next step.

Step 2:     Who are the most important stakeholders?
- Collect on a flipchart, possibly in a mind map

Step 3:     What you have to get right?
- What do you have to get right in order to reach your goal? (Use Post-it notes and cluster them)
- In the first step, each participant writes down the points that

are most important for him or her. After that the participants form small groups (pairs or groups of three or five people, depending on the size of the group) and agree on the three most important points. These are written down on Post-It notes and posted onto a large board.

- Prioritize the contributions by handing out sticky dots and asking the participants to place sticky dots next to their preferred contributions. It usually works quite well if you divide the number of contributions by three and hand out this number of sticky dots per person (e.g. 15 contributions means every person gets five sticky dots.) You can also decide whether you want people to be able to give more than one point to an individual contribution.
- Decide on the most important topics and agree with the group which one will be tackled.

Step 4:     What is already working? (Small groups – one flipchart per group)

- Small groups brainstorm on the clusters identified in step three and write down the most important points that are still working regarding these issues.
- You can support the group's thinking process by asking a scaling question (10 is everything is working and 1 is nothing is working, where are they at the moment and why at this point and not at one)

Step 5:     Future perfect

- An imaginary trip to the future (a possible 10) or the miracle questions
- Write down the most important aspects of a perfect future on Post-It notes.

Step 6:     Scale 1 to miracle

- Scaling Dance: A scale is established on the floor of the meeting room. Participants position themselves on the point of the scale between one and 10 on which they think they are at the moment. They give reasons why they feel they are already at this point. They are then asked to physically take a step in the direction of 10. If you do not have enough space, you can also use a flipchart or figurines on a scale on the table.

- The facilitator then collects answers to the question, "How will you notice that you are one step ahead and what do you need to do to get one step ahead?" on a flipchart

Step 7:    Action Plan:

- The steps developed in step six are again prioritized by sticky dots. Small groups then develop concrete action plans (who, what, how...)
- Afterwards these results can be discussed by the whole group.

## Traps of the methods

When you are clarifying your proposal for what is wanted by the people hiring you, it is very important to clarify whether the results of the meeting are final or whether they are simply the basis of a decision that is taken elsewhere. It is very important to communicate this to the group.

It is also crucial to keep group size in mind. We have some experience with groups of around 30 people who were able to collaborate in this format in the workshop. However, a maximum size of 10 makes more sense.

It is very useful to have two facilitators, one to facilitate and the other to take care of the organizational aspects like visualizing or handing out material. They can take turns in these roles or assign one role for the whole process. The facilitator should definitely have a firm grip on the process and, if necessary, interrupt discussions that are going off on tangents. Otherwise it is very hard to reach results in a short period of time.

Every case is different. PET was devised for situations in which you need to take first concrete steps and have very little time and also needs to generate high buy-in of all stakeholders

## Summary

PET works very well in these specific situations. It can also be modified and combined with other formats, for example World Café and take up one or two days. PET offers great creative potential for workshop design. The prerequisite is that the facilitator is willing to spend preparation time in order to understand the situation of the organization. It is not meant as a recipe book, but as an inspiration for doing the most useful thing for the situation at hand.

# Possible Difficulties

In the following chapter, we would like to describe a few difficulties which may arise when you are facilitating team sessions. Of course, these occur very rarely. However, it still makes sense to think about how you might deal with them, should they happen. Allow me a word of warning: Especially when you have not run many team coaching sessions, you might focus your perception too much on what may go wrong and on all the difficulties you foresee for the session. If you focus too much on what may go wrong, you will become more anxious and increase your perception of any small difficulty and blow it out of proportion – not a good way of creating good conditions for yourself and the team. So read our remarks on how to deal with difficult situations and pack them into your emergency kit and immediately forget that there might be difficult situations ahead. This way, you are prepared, as well as relaxed, and looking forward to your next team coaching session.

## Dealing with difficult participants

If your thinking is solution-focused, no participant is "difficult." As mentioned above, we interpret any behavior of a participant as an offer of co-operation. Naturally, every once in a while we perceive a participant as bothersome. Sometimes a participant also seems to disturb the group. As team coach, we then have to reframe our perception and ask ourselves what the positive intention behind the behavior we perceive as "bothersome" or "disturbing" might be. Sometimes we have to help the group or the respective participant discover what they need or what needs to happen so that the environment can turn into one that no longer makes it necessary for anyone to "be bothered" or "disturbed." The question we primarily use for these types of interventions is "what instead"?

### Negative participants

There are participants who are very critical toward a team coaching process

*If you think solution-focused, no participant is "difficult."*

or team coaching processes in general. They do not believe that anything useful can come out of it. With this kind of expectation they are often looking for confirmation in the session. Every suggestion is not good enough, and every activity is suspected to be a waste of time even before the participant has tried it.

Example 18: **The negative engineer**

> I was facilitating a strategy process for an international engineering company. The most important stakeholders were invited to think about their future communication strategy. Participants were from many countries across the globe. I started by goal setting: "What needs to happen here today so that coming to this workshop was worth your time?" Everybody answered the question – except for a German engineer who said that what we came here to do had been fixed in the agenda and the invitation. He was not in the mood for "games:" the new communication strategy was far too serious a matter. When I asked what needed to happen for him instead of "games," he answered that he needed to see us working seriously on what we came here to do and that not a lot of time should be lost with facilitation blahblah, etc. I asked how he would recognize "serious work." but that was too much for our German engineer. He did not want to comment further. I asked him whether we could continue with the planned process, and he agreed. The rest of the group was very enthusiastic and happy with the process; only our engineer was not joining in.
>
> I asked myself what he might need to be able to participate more energetically, in other words, what was important to him. Since he had not wanted to tell me when I had asked, this was a bit difficult to guess or to find out. I also did not want to focus all my energy on a "negative participant," and thereby take that energy away from the rest of the group. Luckily I remembered that the participant is an experienced professional and adult who probably had good reasons for his behavior. So I continued working with the group and ignored

*the grumpy remarks from the corner in which the engineer had placed himself for the time being.*

*I used a coffee break to start a conversation with him. I confirmed that it was also important for me to have an effective and efficient day with the group. I said that I had heard him say very similar things, e.g. that he wanted an efficient and goal-oriented process. We might, however, have different ideas on what exactly that was – which again is quite normal for people meeting for the first time. And – what a surprise – he agreed. I asked him to be patient and bear with us for a while and also to alert us when we are off track or doing something that makes no sense and make suggestions on how to improve. I told him that it was important for any group to have someone in it who does not fear to give his opinion and who is critical of the process to improve it. In the course of the day, this man was able to make a few very interesting and helpful suggestions which were used positively by both me and the group.*

Giving critical participants the task of being critical participants is sometimes a good chance to help them and the group to profit from each other. On the one hand, you change the perception of the coach from "what a bother" to "he or she has an interesting way of showing his or her cooperation." On the other hand, the critical participant feels that he or she has been taken seriously and his or her needs and concerns have been appreciated.

There are a few traps, however. Sometimes what we are doing actually does not make any sense. We might not have understood what the team wants and what their concerns are. Maybe we missed crucial information or the organization or HR department forgot to tell us something that is important to the team. Or maybe we did not listen well enough. In these situations, you have to go back to zero and think from the beginning. Don't see the "reframe" of a "difficult" participant as a "facilitation trick," but as the sincere quest for finding out what can be useful to the team at any given moment. And if what is useful is not what you planned to do, you have to be flexible and change the plan.

Another trap can be that there are sometimes very different interests of team members represented within a team. It may be that this results in a situation in which it makes more sense for one participant to sabotage the process instead of collaborating on a solution. We do not want to say that it is a good idea to start a team coaching session with this focus – too easily this turns into a self-fulfilling prophecy. In our experience, it makes sense to go back to goal setting when you feel that there are no overlapping interests in a team coaching session. Ask the group: "If this workshop is worth your time, personally, for each one of you, what will be better as a result? What else?" It might be useful to have everybody write down their answers on Post-It notes individually before asking the plenary. You only continue working with the group when you can find a goal that is worth the time for everyone in the room. The worst that can happen is that the group discovers that there are not enough congruent goals to go on – and this is a valuable piece of information. We would then go back to the HR department and the team leaders (if they were not present in the session) and ask what would need to happen to obtain more congruent goals for the team. I might be able to clarify or even change the framework conditions in the organizational environment.

### Negative group – mandated teams

Sometimes the team coach has the impression that the whole group is negative. This happens very rarely when you can clarify what the needs of the group are in interviews with each group member. The cases in which we were confronted with a "negative" group are exclusively from situations in which someone else – and not the team – generated the idea that a team coaching or training session is called for and the team did not agree.

### Example 19: Yet another change!

> At the beginning of my career I was asked to take over presentation training and coaching sessions for a sales team. Their boss had asked one of my network partners and had talked very negatively about their "complete lack of presentation skills." My network partner did not know

*that this boss was known for his temper tantrums and overly critical attitude. He was very unpopular in the organization because he consistently only thought himself as competent and saw everybody else as a "complete waste of space."*

*My network partner – unbeknownst to all this turmoil – called me and asked whether I could run these relatively standard presentation training and coaching sessions for the sales team. He had too much to do. At the start of my career, I was very happy about such an easy and substantial piece of work, so I agreed. I assumed there had been a meeting to clarify the process with the HR-department and maybe even individual representatives of the sales team. Hence, I entered the first session with naïve confidence.*

*Picture my surprise when I arrived and looked into a round of stone-faces. One participant said: "Now let's see what kind of entertainment our boss has provided this time!" People started laughing sarcastically. "Do you know how much presentation experience each and every one of us has?" "There is really nothing that you can teach us or coach us on."*

*I was flabbergasted and the participants probably realized how uncomfortable the situation was for me. This might have eased the tension a little bit. So in my surprise, I asked: "So what makes your boss think that you need a presentation training?" More sarcastic remarks ensued: "When you ask our boss, we probably need training to wash our hands." I sighed: "Oh, I'm sorry – then we are all really at the wrong event." Maybe my unpremeditated sigh made the participants drop their weapons in surprise about my honesty. They started complaining about their boss and told me that it was very difficult to deal with his inability to see their competences. I could very much empathize with them since I was in a very similar situation myself that moment. After a while the group had vented their frustration, and I asked them how they usually dealt with the situation productively.*

*There were the first signs of a willingness to work together and the atmosphere became significantly more productive. One participant said: "There is really no use complaining. We cannot cancel the session, neither can our coach – we would all be in big trouble. And really, it is not the coach's fault." We continued by negotiating about what might happen in the planned sessions so that we would not be wasting everybody's time. The team said they were interested in giving and receiving each other's and my feedback on their presentation skills in real presentations they were planning. They also wanted me to use video (which gave me the opportunity to buy my first camera) to tape and analyze their presentations. We had successfully formed a secret alliance for learning in spite of the circumstances.*

*It is sometimes really hard to see "negative" behavior as an offer of cooperation, but things become a lot easier if you do.*

*After a few sessions, I asked the group whether they wanted to give feedback to their boss on the consequences of his overly critical behavior. However, nobody was confident that this would change anything for the better. The only positive effect I was able to achieve for the team was that I was able to give honest positive feedback on their commitment and performance as presenters to the organization.*

It is sometimes really hard to see "negative" behavior as an offer of cooperation, but things become a lot easier if you do. A "negative" group is at least open and honest and makes it possible for the team coach to start communication about what is needed. The biggest trap in such a situation is for the team coach to take the behavior of the team personally. Even in the unlikely case that the team coach has made a mistake, has not understood what the job is about or not taken concerns seriously enough, it is still better to find out about it before venturing into a session than afterwards in the evaluation sheets. You do not run the risk of spending several days with something that makes no sense at all. We feel strong responsibility when we are taking up the lifetime of our clients with our team coaching measures. If you have 10 people in a 2 day / 16 hour workshop, you are taking up 160 hours, which is 6.66 days in someone's life. We really do not want to waste them. When you are dealing with "mandated teams," i.e. teams which are sent into a team coaching process by their boss or by the HR department and who do not see any need for it themselves, you can use the same tools as when you are working with individual clients. It is important to find out what the clients want to achieve if it is not what the original requestor wants. A useful question for these kinds of situations was developed by Mark McKergow (2002): "Who is a customer for what?"

In contrast to coaching sessions with individual clients, different team members can have varying degrees of willingness to work on a useful goal for the coaching session. It is very important to be sensitive and take care not to lose a participant. If you are too fast, you can lose those who see no need and have no interested in coaching; if you are too slow, you lose the people who have already been able to grasp a sense of the situation. In the worst case, with people who cannot see why they should be in this session at all, we have asked them to look for a space in the room they could use to work on other things rather than getting bored and boring everybody else. When possible, we asked the HR department or the original requestor of the session to agree (without giving individual names). If it is not possible to ask for permission, we would always opt for letting participants use their time in whichever way is most useful for them rather than wasting everybody's time. It takes courage, but nobody has ever criticized us for it after we explained the situation.

## Other possible difficulties

### Attack on the coach

In my 17 years of experience as a coach and team coach, it has only happened twice that participants could not alleviate their frustration other than by attacking us as coaches. The tone was very aggressive and the main concern seemed to be to prove that the coach is a complete idiot. It is very hard to keep calm in such situations, reduce your own stress reaction, and concentrate on the offer of cooperation which is obviously not there. Even in such a situation, it really helps to remember that you are not a complete idiot and that you are in the same boat as the participants.

This situation is specific to work in organizations – it is much less common in therapy situations. When you go to a therapist, you usually think that he or she is competent enough to help you. The question of competence and incompetence does not really arise – if you are unhappy with your therapist, you find a different one. Since solution-focused coaching uses techniques originally developed by solution-focused therapy, there are no real precedents or techniques we can steal from therapy.

*Example 20:* **The coach as idiot**

> *Mr. Grabert was grumpy. Again, such a useless, stupid coaching session. His whole desk was full of important work. It was shortly before the end of the fiscal year, and his bonus depended on his ability to close an important deal before that. Maybe there was a way to shorten the session if he could curb the coach's enthusiasm. He entered the workshop room with a frosty demeanor. Many of his colleagues were already there – Grabert was sure that they would also appreciate a shorter (or no) session. After the team coach had welcomed everybody, the following dialogue ensued:*
>
> *Team coach: "I looked at the minutes of our last coaching session …"*
>
> *Grabert: "Oh, yes? And did you understand anything? My impression was that you did not. Admit it – you have no clue when it comes to our business. You are just a hired training girl in a suit ready to cash in on your daily rates."*

Exercise 9: **The coach as idiot**

> Think about what you would answer in such a situation – however it might have arisen. Identify at least seven possibilities so that you are prepared if you ever get into such a situation. Rest assured, however, that such a conflict in the vast majority of cases has nothing to

do with your qualification as coach, but rather is a result of difficult interactions before. Remember, you might not be the best coach in the world, but you are the only one who is there.

_____

_____

_____

_____

_____

_____

_____

_____

_____

_____

_____

_____

_____

_____

_____

Here are our seven possibilities:

## Counterattack

What? A counterattack by a solution-focused coach? You cannot be serious! Did you not just say that it was all about cooperation? Yes, it is about cooperation. However, there are business cultures in which the solution-focused "Aikido" method of gentle and productive interaction is perceived as too soft and is not taken seriously. A team coach who cannot stand his or her ground when attacked in this way will have difficulties in achieving a productive result. In these few cases, a counterattack can make sense. What is important is to return to cooperation very quickly. This is almost like a ritual, a duel: everybody shows their weapons. After it has been established that the other is a worthy opponent, and you belong to the same class of serious thugs, you can go on to plan the next robbery. When we were running a conflict coaching process in Dubai, the group told us that a first step in solving a conflict situation could also be to start yelling and shouting at your opponent. They thought this behavior would create respect and the willingness to cooperate. Of course, this is not our preferred solution, but if called for, why not? In our case this strategy could play out like this:

> *A team coach who cannot stand his or her ground when attacked in this way will have difficulties in achieving a productive result.*

> Grabert: "Oh, yes? And did you understand anything? My impression was that you did not. Admit it – you have no clue when it comes to our business. You are just a hired training girl in a suit ready to cash in on your daily rates."

> Team coach: "Mr. Grabert, if comments like this really impressed me, I would probably really have no clue about your business – do you have another one?"

## Columbo method

Many over 30-year-old readers will know Peter Falk as Inspector Columbo.

The character is an absent-minded homicide cop who solves many cases by feigning to walk out the door after he is done questioning a suspect. The suspect lets down his guard and thinks that the interrogation is over. Inspector Columbo turns around, still pretending to be absent-minded and confused and asks one question that will decide the case. This is why feigned confusion is called the "Columbo Method." This method works especially well because it offers an alternative to the instinctive "fight or flight" mechanism that kicks in with most of us when we are in stressful situations.

> Grabert: "Oh, yes? And did you understand anything? My impression is that you did not. Admit it – you have no clue when it comes to our business. You are just a hired training girl in a suit ready to cash in on your daily rates."
>
> Team coach: "Uh-hum, yes. I also really like my suit. Now I'm a little bit confused. What does all of that have to do with our minutes?"
>
> To the other participants: Let's go on, shall we?"

## Answering with a question

The traditional method, used in solution-focus, is to step back and ask about the goal or those who may have coping questions.

> Grabert: "Oh, yes? And did you understand anything? My impression is that you did not. Admit it – you have no clue when it comes to our business. You are just a hired training girl in a suit ready to cash in on your daily rates."
>
> Team coach: "I am really sorry that you feel this way. What could we do under the given circumstances so that this is worth your time?"

The question of competence or incompetence of the team coach is not discussed.

## Conflicts take precedence

In European systemic consulting there is a saying: "Disturbances take precedence!" We do not think that this is really the case. When you adopt this adage, it is all too easy to focus on all the factors that make a successful coaching process difficult. Nevertheless, it is not the adage itself, but the systemic process which consultants suggest that is very useful. The behavior of the participant is labeled "a disturbance in the interaction" and not classified as a form of aggression. A "disturbance" is much less dramatic than a conflict and takes up much less attention. It is simply normal that human relationships and interactions are sometimes "disturbed" and not running smoothly.

> Grabert: "Oh, yes? And did you understand anything? My impression is that you did not. Admit it – you have no clue when it comes to our business. You are just a hired training girl in a suit ready to cash in on your daily rates."
>
> Team coach: "Oh – it looks like we're having a bit of a glitch in the process. Actually, I wanted to discuss the goal of this meeting with you, but this doesn't seem to be the right thing at the moment."
>
> To all participants: "It seems to me that it would be useful to look at this glitch before working on the results we want to come away with. Would that be okay with everyone? Mr. Grabert – what is important for you at the moment?"

## What is still working well?

A solution-focused way of dealing with such "disturbances" or "glitches" is to look for exceptions and resources. There is obviously little confidence that something can happen in this coaching session which is useful for the team. A prerequisite for using this solution-focused way of dealing with such a situation is recognizing and acknowledging that the process or relationship isn't working smoothly at the moment.

> Grabert: "Oh, yes? And did you understand anything? My impression is that you did not. Admit it – you have no clue when it comes to our business. You are just a hired training girl in a suit ready to cash in on your daily rates."

*Team coach: "Oh, I'm really sorry – our collaboration doesn't seem to be working very well at the moment, does it? However, I do think if anything is to come out of this session, we have to collaborate and come to a productive working relationship. It would really help if we all are confident that we can achieve something useful today."*

*To everybody: "Would it be okay if we started by spending some time on this?"*

*The team coach then takes a flipchart and jots down a scale of 1 to 10. 10 means that the team is very confident that this team coaching session will have useful results and one is the opposite. The team members now rate their confidence by posting sticky dots or marking a cross on that scale anonymously (the team coach looks out of the window during the process).*

*Team coach: "Let us first look at why some of you are not at 1. What is already happening in our coaching session, something that I am doing or something that you as a team are doing, that gives you confidence that this can be useful?"*

*These answers are collected on a flipchart. Afterwards, the team coach elicits answers on what X+1 would look like. What would need to happen so that the team can be a little bit more confident that the results of the process will be useful? Again, it helps to create one flipchart for what the team will be doing, if it is more confident that something can come out of the sessions and what the coach will be doing when the team is one step higher on the confidence scale.*

## What was that all about?

Very seldom, there will be cases in which you have situations where one participant in the workshop isn't able to behave in such a way that the other participants to not feel extremely disturbed by his or her behavior. This does not happen often, and in our case it has never happened in business situations. We do know these kinds of situations from our work with high school students and workshops for unemployment agencies. Our experience transferred to our example could look like this:

> *Grabert: "Oh, yes? And did you understand anything? My impression is that you did not. Admit it – you have no clue when it comes to our business. You are just a hired training girl in a suit ready to cash in on your daily rates."*

> *Team coach: "Mr. Grabert, what was that all about? You're obviously not willing to collaborate constructively here. Do us all a favor and go back to your office and work on something that is useful for you. I suggest we meet with your boss and the HR department later on to agree on how we should proceed afterwards."*

## The seventh method

The seventh method is the method: "It always depends…" Continue thinking about what kind of solutions you would feel happy with and how you could feel comfortable in difficult situations. I'm sure you will find your very own "seventh method."

### Endless chatter

Sometimes you have people in workshops who talk a lot. Their motto seems to be: "Everything has been said but not by everybody." Therefore, they busily repeat what has already been said or illustrate points that have been previously mentioned with their own lengthy examples that nobody is really interested in. The other participants begin to roll their eyes and become annoyed. Sometimes this kind of behavior can even get on the nerves of the most patient team coach.

It is important to differentiate these two things: Is the participant getting on your nerves only? Then it might be best to mentally take a "patience-pill" and remind yourself that work is sometimes work. If the participant is getting on the nerves of other participants or even the whole team, then it might be helpful to launch an appreciative attempt to rein in the chatter.

All methods which deprive the chatterbox of their audience are usually useful: small group work, peer work or individual work. We have created especially good experiences with cascading groups: you pose a question and everybody thinks about the answer individually first. Next, you condense the most important aspects of your answer together with a partner. Then you form small groups of four people who write down the most important results on a maximum of three Post-It Notes.

We don't think that exposing the chatterbox in front of the group or making him or her lose face makes sense. Sometimes it is useful to spend some time with such people during the break and listen to what they have to say. It also helps to remind yourself that some people learn by verbalizing what they think. Usually chatterboxes do not have negative intentions – they want to contribute and help people have fun, and they think their discoveries are important and want to share them. We've also found that recognizing the expertise of the chatterbox can help. We have asked them during the break whether they would mind holding back what they have to say to give the other participants the chance to think for themselves or to generate answers since they seem to need more time.

## The aquarium

Sometimes you are confronted with the opposite problem. You enter the room as a team coach, and one by one of the participants start arriving. They do not

*Everything has been said but not by everybody.*

say anything except for a mumbled "morning." The answers to any questions of the team coach are short and there are long breaks in the conversation. You feel like you are sitting in a goldfish glass among the fish.

Exercise 10: **We have ways of making you talk**

> At this point you already have quite some exercise in devising possible reactions. Invent at least four ways of activating the participants or helping them to contribute.

## Pair work or small groups

Devise a really good question and ask the participants to work on this question in small groups or pairs. Tell them beforehand how to document the result: on Post-It notes, in a role-play or on the flipchart.

## Paradoxical silence

The team coach takes up the language of the team, stops speaking and from now on continues working nonverbally by gestures and mimics, like a pantomime. Here she writes a question and a number of minutes on the flipchart. He or she signals like a pantomime that now everybody should start working on this question individually. If a participant starts to talk here she signals him or her to be quiet. After a while everybody will probably want to start talking.

## Patiently count to 300

Patiently accepting the fact that there is silence is not always easy. However, it can be a good method to warm up the group. Usually, the silence is not the problem. The problem is that the coach starts thinking about why the group is silent and gets entangled in his or her own interpretations of the silence. Counting to 300 is sometimes more useful than trying to entertain the group or "fill" the silence.

## Ask what the matter is

You can simply ask why everybody is so quiet. It might be that yesterday was the night of the annual company party, an important football game was lost by the local team, or there were other reasons why everybody didn't sleep well. Maybe there is also an important reason that you can deal with in the team coaching session.

### Dealing with strong emotions

"The whole world is a very narrow bridge and the main thing is not to be frightened" is a beautiful old Jewish saying. Human beings have strong emotions when something is important to them. We do not ignore this fact in solution-focused work: emotions simply happen and belong to any process. The difference to traditional work is that we do not focus on the expression of emotions. They are simply there and in most cases they do not get in the way of the work. Insoo Kim Berg is said to have mentioned in a conversation with a woman who was very sad and could not stop crying: "You know, it is possible to cry and think at the same time." So if somebody becomes emotional in a few workshops or somebody is angry or sad, then your main task as team coach is not to be frightened and keep focusing on the good in the working relationship: the goal, exceptions, and resources. It is very helpful to have an attitude of "it is completely normal that you feel this way, these things happen."

> *The whole world is a very narrow bridge and the main thing is not to be frightened*

Example 21: **Anger and frustration**

> *Everything in the company was going downhill. Salaries were no longer as good as they had been. The food in the cafeteria had gotten worse. The company was hiring more and more temporary people and was giving out less and less normal contracts. The leadership team of this company was fed up with everything. The last thing that they wanted was a coaching session to think about how to lead their people. During the whole day they kept talking about how it was really impossible to lead people well under these kinds of conditions. They were simply upset.*

> *After the whole group had started another round of complaining, I asked the team whether we should plan some time to talk about "leading in difficult situations." I was very surprised to hear that they were not at all interested in talking about this topic. They all thought this would not change anything. The conditions of the company were dictated by economic circumstances and they would not be able to do anything about that. I asked the team how we could deal with this instead and how we could deal with their understandable, yet not very productive, desire to have time to complain every once in a while.*

*In the morning we had talked about how team members notice when they have a good team leader. One answer was that the leader would take time to listen to them and acknowledge and recognize their concerns and complaints. They had named this: "Sometimes being a wailing wall." We then agreed that also a team coaching session can be used to express frustration, complaints, and concerns about the situation and that it would be useful for them if I acted as their "wailing wall." I should simply listen patiently and remind them to return to more productive issues after 5 minutes.*

## Summary

Dealing with difficult participants
- Negative participants
- Negative group – mandated teams

Other possible difficulties
- Attack on the coach
  - Counterattack
  - Columbo method
  - Answering with a question
  - Conflicts take precedence
  - What is still working well?
  - What was that all about?
  - The seventh method
- Endless chatter
- The aquarium
  - Pair work or small groups
  - Paradoxical silence
  - Patiently count to 300
  - Ask what the matter is
- Dealing with strong emotions

# Typical requests for team coaching

## Conflict

### The basics

When conflicts arise in the team coaching process between team members, or if the conflict is the reason for the team coaching process, the first important question is who are the best people to start solving it? If you separate the conflict parties from the team and try to solve the conflict with these parties, you signalize that the rest of the team

> *An important question: Who are the best people to solve the conflict?*

members have nothing to do with it. Both conflict parties are identified as "the problem."

If you try to solve the conflict with the whole team, you run the risk of having the conflict parties lose face in front of the whole group. An isolated conflict that does not have a lot to do with the whole group can also steer a great deal of energy and attention away from what is important to the group.

It is difficult to say which procedure is best. In any case, it is important to keep these possible dynamics in mind. As with any team coaching process, it is very important for the team coach to stay multi-partial in conflict situations. Every team member should be able to assume that the team coach is on his or her side. This is easiest if the coach can sympathize with the different perceptions and does not try to judge them: it is what it is. The coach should try to speak the language of all conflict parties. He or she may need to invent language which gives every conflicted party the feeling that they have been understood. The team coach listens especially carefully for possible joint goals, exceptions, and resources. Here is an example in which conflict at the end of the team coaching session helped the team to get to an even better solution:

*Example 22:* **It's not that life's a piece of cake**

*Ms. Miller felt that she was being treated unfairly. Ms. Faber always got the more interesting projects. Ms. Faber mainly had to deal with IT (databases and project documentation). Ms. Faber had promised to receive training from Ms. Miller to be able to deal with these kinds of tasks. However, that training had not happened in the last two years.*

*The team coaching process was about developing strategies for the next year, deciding who would work together with whom and what priorities should be. During the whole process, Ms. Miller had not talked about her desire to do something other than databases and pro-ject documentation. She seemed a bit shy but positive and interested in results. When the tasks and responsibilities were being distributed at the end of the workshop, everybody simply assumed that Ms. Miller would continue to deal with documentation and databases. When she realized this, she lost her temper.*

*Ms. Miller: "Yeah, sure, me again. Right. Great! I will probably be spending the rest of my life programming stupid databases just be-cause everybody else is too lazy or stupid to learn how to do this. Ms. Faber – you have been promising me for ages that you will let me show you. I am fed up!!"*

*Ms. Faber: "Ms. Miller, you know well that I did not have any time to get trained on this. Do you think we like looking into your sour face when we ask you to program a database for us? It's not that life's a piece of cake!"*

*Chef: "Ms. Miller, Ms. Faber – that's really not what we are here for!"*

*Team coach: "Just a moment. Let me see if I got that right: Ms. Miller, you would like us to take into account that you would like to do other things that just database programming when we assign tasks, right?"*

*Ms. Miller: "Exactly, but …"*

*Team coach (interrupts): "Okay, good. Ms. Faber, if I understand you correctly, it is important for you to recognize that all team members do* things that are not their favorite tasks and that everybody should be a good sport not get on other people's nerves with their bad moods."

Ms. Faber: "Yes, correct and Ms. Miller is ..."

Team coach (interrupts): "We have about 1.5 hours left. I do not think that we have time here to talk about what went wrong in the past. But we can take care to see that it will be better for everybody in the future. So please excuse my interrupting you a bit brusquely. If you are interested we can talk about what happened between the three of us, if you want. But now let us use the remaining time to think about a way of distributing tasks that everybody is happy with, okay?"

Ms. Faber and Ms. Miller: "Of course ..., yeah ..., you're right ..., I'm sorry ..., the main thing is that we will find a better solution for the future."

Team coach: "So the way we just suggested to distribute the tasks does not seem optimal. What about the other team members: would it be okay with you if we spent some time thinking about which criteria tell you that the tasks have been distributed well. It would be nice if everybody could have fun with most of the tasks assigned to them, wouldn't it?"

Team: "Sure ..., yes, okay ..., you're right."

Team coach: "Mr. Boss, are you okay with that, too?"

Boss: "Well, our previous solution doesn't really seem to work anyway"

Team coach: "Then let's get down to business. We have been working with scales the whole day. Let us first define what a 10 of a good task distribution is. Then let's see what we already have and then continue thinking about what the steps would be for an even better task distribution. Okay?"

Team: "Okay, let's roll!"

Team coach: "Let's spend 45 min. on this and then we have another 45 min. for more task distribution."

Team: "Sure""

*Team coach: "Please take five Post-It notes each and write down five criteria that tell you that you have a good task distribution in your team. How would you know that your task distribution is at a 10 on the scale?"*

*The team worked for 40 minutes and found that many of the criteria they had for a good task distribution (oriented to the competencies of each team member, clarity of priorities, information routes in case of changes, etc.) had already been fulfilled. What was not working just yet was training each other and standing in for each other in case of absences. Also, the team members did not yet dare to talk about what they liked doing and what they did not like doing so much. It seemed that Ms. Miller's outbreak had opened the possibility for the whole team to talk about personal preferences. The whole team was very happy with the new solution.*

*Team coach: "I am very impressed with how you want to take care of each other in this team. It is not only important to you that you do your work in a professional way and that you distribute work fairly, but you also want to take care of individual preferences. Thank you, Ms. Miller und Ms. Faber, for enabling us to have this discussion. If you had not talked about this, the result would not have been as effective."*

## Steps of conflict mediation

Just as in team coaching sessions, conflict mediation never follows the exact same process. The process always has to be adapted to the concerned in-dividuals and there is no pre-described sequence of steps. It sometimes happens that you need to take a loop back to the step that you had already talked about previously. The topic of solution-focused conflict mediation has been dealt with extensively in Fredrike Bannink's wonderful book "Solution focused Mediation" (Bannink, 2010). Here are some possible steps, which you will also find discussed this way or in a similar way in her book:

*Drama and conflict are almost magical magnets for our attention.*

## Establishing and maintaining a good working relationship

When you are dealing with conflict, it is especially important to establish and create a useful working relationship – not only between the coach and concerned parties but also between the conflicted parties themselves. This is sometimes not easy. Feelings have been hurt and communication is obstructed. It is hard for the conflicted parties to regain confidence that a good solution is possible. Drama and conflict are almost magical magnets for our attention. Remember the last time you had a serious conflict and remember how difficult it was to think about anything else. It was as if the thought of the conflict dismissed all other thoughts you might have had.

Apart from the normal solution-focused possibilities for creating a good working relationship, such as normalizing (meaning it is completely normal for everybody to feel what they are feeling in this moment), Fredrike Bannink has

*What do you need to speak about here today so that you can have a productive and future-oriented conversation?*

developed another method. She calls it the "Maori Method." Apparently, it is customary in the Maori culture that every participant in the meeting gets a chance to speak up once at the beginning of the meeting. He or she can speak as long as he or she wants, but then has to sit down and cannot reply to anything that is being said until the round is finished. This leads to everybody saying only what is really important to them. Also, people tend not to say anything too offensive because other people could react to this and they would then not be able to defend themselves. A solution-focused way to use the "Maori-method" is to ask: "What do you need to speak about here today so that you can have a productive and future-oriented conversation?"

## Goal – goal behind the goal

"What is better for all conflicted parties when the conflict has been dissolved?" Using this or a similar future-oriented question, we try to find out what the world of the conflicted parties will look like when the conflict has disappeared. The question serves to turn the attention of the conflicted parties to things that exist outside of the conflict. It generates hope that a life without the conflict is possible. This can only work if we can describe what would be there instead. Other questions could be:

- Suppose your conflict was solved, just like this, what would that look like? What would be possible then that is not possible now? What else?

- Imagine ... you go home after this meeting. The meeting was very useful for you. So you go home and you do whatever you plan to do for the rest of the day. Sometime in the evening you get tired and go to sleep. In the middle of the night a miracle happens, and the miracle is that the conflict has disappeared into thin air... just like that. Since you are sleeping you do not know that a miracle happened – and nobody tells you, either. How would you start noticing the next morning that miracle must have happened? Who else will notice? How? What will they notice? What will you be doing differently? What else?

- When your conflict is solved, what will be better? What exactly? What will be better for you (party 1)? What for you (party 2)? What do you think will be better for party 1? What do you think will be better for party 2? ... And when this happens what else will be better?

Afterwards you can start by setting goals for the coaching process at hand: "What needs to happen here today so that we can take a small step in the right direction?"

## Exceptions and resources

Once you have elicited the goal behind the goal, you can start discovering exceptions and resources. You can either do that by using a scaling question, where 10 is somewhere between reaching the end goal after the miracle (if people already have a lot of confidence), or as small as "it is a little bit more likely that you can take a small step in order to start working together again."

The next questions could be:

- When was the last time that the situation was a little bit like after the miracle?
- How high was that on the scale?
- What became possible for you?
- What exactly did party 1 or party 2 do in this moment?
- What did each of them contribute?
- There was a time before the conflict – how was your relationship then?
- What exactly did you do when it was better?
- How did other people notice that it was better?
- What else?

> It is most important to find something that helps parties to move out of the perception that the other person is only doing things to bother them.

### Next steps

At the end of the mediation process the parties agree on experiments, actions, and first or next steps that could lead to an improvement.

### Experiments

Experiments offer good possibilities for the parties to venture gently into a new reality which includes hope for better collaboration. Sometimes it is not easy to imagine that healing a work relationship is possible (and even possible quickly) after so much excitement and conflict. The parties in conflict sometimes feel like a quick solution signifies a failure to recognize that there was a lot of suffering during the time of the conflict. This is why as coach you should try and go slow and never express more confidence than the clients themselves.

Here are some interesting experiments:

- Observe closely and notice everything which goes in the right direction. Please report these instances to the coach in the next session – this is necessary because we have to find out exactly what you want instead of the conflict.

- Throw a coin every evening – heads means that you will conduct yourself the same way as you always do, tails means you behave as if the miracle had already happened.

- Whenever you see that the other party is doing something that they should continue to be doing, put a small flower on their desk.

- Make an attempt to say something positive about your colleague in front of others at least four times next week. The special challenge is that you have to mean it.

## Agreements and actions

When both parties are no longer extremely emotionally involved and are confident that the conflict can be solved, both can make contributions about how they want to behave in the future so that a conflict like this is avoided or the existing conflict is solved.

To start the discussion you could ask:

- When you are looking back on this time two years from now and everything went in a way that you can actually be proud of yourself and how you conducted yourself, what will you be saying then about your attitude and your behavior during this time?

The coach asks both parties what their plan is for improving the situation and asks the other party if they agree or if there is anything else that they need and vice versa.

### Example 23: **The files are in a mess**

*Team coach: "I think we are now clear about how both of you would like each other's behavior to be in the future. Ms. Rutter, you are at a 4. Ms. Andres, you are at a 5. Suppose both of you are one step higher on the scale. What will you be doing then that you are not doing or doing less of today?"*

*Ms. Andres:* "I heard Ms. Rutter say it is important for her that she can find everything when somebody calls. I could take the last 10 minutes of my work and try to put everything back and write a quick note for Ms. Rutter."

*Team coach:* "Ms. Rutter, what will you do when you are step higher on your scale?"

*Ms. Rutter:* "Instead of getting terribly upset when I cannot find something, I will write a text message to Ms. Andres asking her where I might find it."

*Team coach:* "Ms. Andres – does this work you, if Ms. Rutter writes you a text message in these cases?"

*Ms. Andres:* "We can at least try it. And also, I can influence this. If I do not have time to put everything back or to explain where I put things, I will get more text messages. At least it is worth a try."

*Team coach:* "How confident are you on a scale of 0 to 10, where 10 means that you are very confident, that this can bring an improvement and you can actually implement this step?"

*Ms. Andres:* "A 6."

*Ms. Rutter:* "Also around a 6."

*Team coach:* "What makes you confident?"

> *The conflicted parties sometimes feel like a quick solution signifies a failure to recognize that there was a lot of suffering during the time of the conflict. This is why as coach you should try and go slow and never express more confidence than the clients themselves.*

The next steps and agreements should be things that both parties actually want to implement and that make both parties confident that they can lead to an improvement. Talk is cheap in these circumstances. It is most important to find something that helps parties to move out of the perception that the other person is only doing things to bother them. In these situations, it is also possible to ask what will happen if the parties do not stick to their agreements and design a strategy on how to get back on track. This way the parties can prepare to deal with setbacks without questioning the success of what has already happened.

Exercise 11: **De-escalation**

> Ben Furman and Tapani Ahola developed a very nice exercise for teams who are often in conflict situations with other teams. This exercise contrasts the "normal" or usual behavior of teams which team members often display when they are in conflict with other people, who then become "the enemy," with a more constructive way of dealing with inter-group conflict. You can suggest this exercise when you see a similar dynamic happening. First split the group into two small groups. Group A leaves the room and thinks about the faults of Group B. Group A then enters the room. You facilitate the following typical dialogue (maybe supported by a visualization on a flipchart). The objective is to simulate the typical escalation process and a conflict – try to have fun with the group in role-playing the road to conflict.

Here is the process:

1. Group A blames Group B for something.
2. Group B denies it.
3. Group A finds examples to support the blame.
4. Group B blames these examples on the conditions and/or the environment.
5. Group A develops an explanation for the unprofessional behavior of Group B.
6. Group B develops an explanation about why Group A accused Group B this unfairly.
7. Group A threatens Group B with consequences.
8. Group B threatens Group A with consequences if they don't stop accusing Group B.
9. Group A leaves the room.

While Group A is outside, you explain to Group B how you can react constructively to criticism, be it justified or not. Again, you can write down these points on a flipchart.

1. Listen.
2. Express empathy – maybe even say you are sorry.
3. Ask what the other group wants instead.
4. Negotiate.
5. Agree on a first step.

Group A comes back to the room. This time Group B reacts constructively. This conversation is normally much calmer and is more goal-oriented. Most of the time you do not have to say much about why it makes more sense to react to criticism as was demonstrated in the second example.

## Bullying / Mobbing

There is not a lot of solution-focused literature on the topics of "bullying" or "mobbing." This is probably because solution-focused work strives to describe problems in such a way that they are perceived as solvable and changeable. "Bullying / Mobbing" always sounds very severe rather than changeable or chronic. Many issues which would probably fall under the term "bullying" or "mobbing" in other consulting approaches might be dealt with under the headings of: "a positive work atmosphere," "generating value out of diversity," "dealing with misunderstandings" etc. – depending on the issue at hand.

However, sometimes we are asked to submit proposals on the topic of "the prevention of bullying or mobbing." Sue Young has developed very good model (Young, 2009) for schools. This has not been transferred into the business world, yet we think that this could be done with some changes. The following presents two possible applications:

### Prevention of bullying

Suppose you, a solution-focused consultant, are asked by a company to support them with a program to prevent bullying or mobbing. Of course, you will first find out what your possible customers will see happening in their company instead of mobbing or bullying. What exactly is the picture of a work environment where no employee is being bullied by your client? Such requests usually originate in the HR-department, the training and development department, the works council or other union representatives. Here is a possible process for solution-focused consulting in the case of the prevention of bullying or mobbing:

1. Clarifying the proposal with the possible client
   a. What exactly does a work atmosphere look like which makes bullying or mobbing unlikely or impossible?
   b. Which of these factors already exist in your company?
   c. What does the company already do in order to support this atmosphere?
   d. Which ideas are there to do more of that and what else can you do in addition?
2. Integration of important stakeholders
   a. Communicating the goal (for example, a safe and inspiring work atmosphere)
   b. Workshops with the stakeholders scaling the work atmosphere
   c. Generating further ideas
3. Planning the implementation of the next steps
4. Implementation
5. Communication of results: What was done? How did the employees react? etc.

There are some current approaches to anti-bullying or anti-mobbing which are very different or even diametrically opposed to solution-focused approaches. Traditional HR or talent development sometimes assumes that in order to tackle any issue, the first step absolutely needs to be raising awareness of the problem. Without raising awareness, no risk or problem can be dealt within this view. When you are dealing with such a potential client, you sometimes have to try to convince the client that the program, which does not even mention the words bullying or mobbing, can actually be as successful or even more successful than traditional awareness raising programs. Sue Young quotes several statistics which can help here. In her research, she found that traditional mobbing or bullying prevention in schools usually leads to more bullying or mobbing. The reason here can be that after awareness raising, conflicts which usually would have been labeled mere conflicts are then labeled bullying or mobbing. Of course, sometimes focusing on a problem also creates a sort of confirmation bias, where you suddenly only see what you are awareness is focused on. For example, when you want to buy a certain brand of car, you seem to only see this brand. Sometimes focusing on the problem creates exactly that problem.

Another self-fulfilling prophecy in companies is their desire to measure qualitative programs quantitatively. This desire can lead to asking you to conduct an employee opinion survey after your program. Sadly, most employee opinion surveys lead to increased dissatisfaction of employees. Employees imagine the most beautiful, friendliest, and productive company as their 10 on the scale and forget that this company can never exist. They then compare their own, not so perfect company to this ideal. This unreal discrepancy then leads to disappointment and dissatisfaction that had not been there before. Of course, it is legitimate for a company to want to know whether their programs are successful or not. As a consultant, you can try to introduce the possibility of qualitative interviews instead of anonymous surveys to measure success. An independent interviewer can then talk to employees in a standardized format, or conduct standardized interviews that ask about what contributes to their satisfaction with the work atmosphere and what still might need to be done.

## Concrete allegations of bullying

In the case of concrete allegations of bullying, Sue Young suggests something similar to the so-called "no blame approach." If a child or parents feel that a child is being bullied, Sue Young works with a "support group." The procedure is as follows:

1. A solution-focused interview is conducted with the child in question. The consultant asks who the child perceives as difficult, which children are his or her friends, and who would she like to have as friends. The child is also asked about which children are often around when there are situations in which he or she feels bullied.

2. The children who are mentioned by the concerned child are invited for a group conversation. This group conversation is about getting together as a group in order to help the child who is feeling bullied to feel happier in school. Every one of the children find something concrete they can do in order to help the child. During this group meeting there is no differentiation between the children were difficult for the concerned child and those he or she would like to have as his or her friends.

3. After a few weeks there is another conversation with the child in question about what has changed for the better and how he or she has been able to react.

4. Another meeting is called with the support group on the same topic.

We do not know whether or how this kind of procedure can be used for adults, as well. Allegations of mobbing or bullying can happen in very different circumstances and can have very different backgrounds in the business world. The range is from situations in which an employee is very unpopular and suffers because of that, to conflicts in which employees try to get the other to leave the company, or even in situations in which allegations of mobbing or bullying become tools in a power struggle.

When your clients are adults, you probably have to pay closer attention to the goals of each concerned person. Only in the case of one person feeling very unhappy in the social life of the team would a process like the one suggested for schools by Sue Young be suitable.

The solution-focused approach is again very different from the process other consulting firms would suggest in these cases. We would never ask a concerned person to write a bullying diary in which he or she writes down all the terrible things happening to him or her. We also think that the assumption that people decidedly aim at the psychological destruction of other people is not useful if you want to find a solution in which everybody can live and work together afterwards. Of course, this does not mean that this is never the case, but the assumption leads to assigning blame, to a perpetrator and a victim, and this division of the world is usually an obstacle on your way to a solution.

Again – you do not have any of experience trying to use Sue Young's approach for adults. However, we are very interested in this topic and would like to encourage our readers to contact us if they have questions or experiences.

Another interesting approach is "restorative" justice which focuses on creating a good future after an event in which someone became a victim as a consequence of someone else's behavior. I strongly advocate not trying to divide the world into perpetrators and victims, but if this is the construction of both "victim" and "perpetrator" restorative justice is a good starting point because it focuses on the future and on what needs to happen so that it can be a good future for all.

## Teambuilding

*Situations*

In companies, teams often form or reform: the team has a new superior, your team members have joined another team, or two or more teams are merged and roles and responsibilities have to be reassigned. The team coach is called to help the team get to know each other quickly and pave the way for smooth collaboration.

*Structure*

The structure we use in the team coaching process regarding teambuilding is very similar to the structure we use in other processes.

## Clarifying the contract

The first step is a conversation with the (new) superior of the (new) team about the tasks and goals of the team has and what the team needs to get right in the next couple of months. We ask what makes the superior confident that these tasks can be successfully done by the team. We also ask which resources the superior is already seeing: what does he or she appreciate about the team members that he or she already knows? If he or she selected the team members, what were his or her criteria?

## Interviews

We conduct interviews with team members.

Questions can be:

- What does good teamwork look like to you?
- How do you want your new team to work? What would you like to accomplish?
- What is your experience in building teams?
- When this happened before, what worked well?
- What would you like to contribute to this new team?
- What do you have to get right when you are building the foundation of your team? What should you and your other team members take care of?

## Workshop

The workshop depends on the issues the team members have at this time. Sometimes the focus is more strongly on planning for the future and sometimes it is more about getting to know each other and building trust. These workshops are very individual. Here are a few exercises which we have used in such situations:

### Getting-to-know-each other-bingo

You create a bingo table of four by four fields. You write an unusual experience, strength or something interesting in the life of a person into each field. This might look like this:

| Jumped off a plane with a parachute | Play piano | Am SAP Specialist | Had guinea pigs as pets |
|---|---|---|---|
| Rode on an elephant | Have been on more than three continents | Speak more than 2 languages | Am a good salesperson |
| Love Powerpoint | Have grandchildren | Have run a marathon | Love cats |
| Love Hunde | Have been on a mountain higher than 4000 m | Am a good cook | Was prom queen |

Every team member tries to get a straight line ticking the boxes – just like in bingo – writing in names of people who have had the respective experience. The person who has four boxes in a row first, wins. Of course, to find out, you have to talk to as many people as possible in a short period of time. This game is also very nice as a game accompanying an evening at the bar.

## Mixed Interviews

If a team has been merged from two or more teams, you can also ask small mixed groups to interview each other and then introduce him or her to the plenary. Useful questions can be:

- What was one of your biggest successes in the last years?
- How did you manage those successes?
- What would you like to see us doing in our new team?
- What are you really good at and what do you really dislike?

## Resource-board

The resource-board is a very nice way of visualizing team resources. Every team member writes their names on Post-It notes about which situations or questions they can be asked about and are willing to help. These Post-It notes are glued to a board or a wall. Most often you get a very nice picture of the competences in the team. Sometimes you even realize that something is missing (for example, the team is using SAP, but there is really no specialist); the superior can think about who might want training or if there is anyone who could be a resource for the team.

### Fun activities

Fun activities are very nice way to get to know each other outside of the company. For example, you can cook something together or you can go on hiking trip or engage in other sports. There are many options for company outings. When choosing such an activity, it is very useful to look for an event company who is not trying to interpret the team's behavior. Fun activities are most useful if people can spend time together, chat, and be themselves. For us, it is also always important that nobody needs to go out of their comfort zone. Even if the group has only one couch potato, I would not go rock climbing, for example.

### What do we want to keep?

Asking each part of the new team what their positive experiences were with the old team can be a powerful question. You can have storytelling rounds which everybody can tell their war stories of team successes. The consultant asks about what made the team successes possible and how this can also happen in the new team.

You can visualize the results on a flipchart under the heading of: "What we love about teamwork."

### Criteria of good task assignment and distribution

When tasks are being reassigned in a new team, you often get conflicts (see the example above). Nobody wants to get rid of responsibilities that they liked, and things that are not so popular should be distributed equally, etc. If the team can influence the task assignment and the superior does not decide to do this him or herself, it is very important to clarify what can be decided by the team and what has already been decided.

Discussing the criteria of a good distribution of tasks before entering into the main discussion often makes things a lot easier. Sometimes even adults think that everything can be handled in a 100% fair way, which is a bit unrealistic. If you think about the "good enough" criteria of good distribution of tasks, people become more realistic.

A good visualization is also crucial to a clear task distribution process. Having huge walls of paper, multicolored markers, and multicolored Post-It notes etc. really helps to create clarity.

## Follow-up

In teambuilding processes it is very useful to conduct a follow-up session after around three months. In the follow-up session, you ask what is better and what is working well, and what the team did to make that happen. This way team cohesion is strengthened and the team understands and can build on their teambuilding performance.

Useful questions can be:

- What is better?
- What is working really well?
- What did you notice about your colleagues that you really like?
- What do you want to keep doing?
- What are you definitely going to do again the way you did it now if you should ever be in a situation to contribute to that new team again?

# Virtual teams

*What are global virtual teams?*

In many global corporations, teams no longer consist of team members who are located in one location; the team is often distributed over many countries and possibly many time zones. The advantage for the company is that they can react faster to customer requests and they can always be reached by various customers from all over the world. The fact that you can unite talents from many different countries in one project or one team is also very useful. Companies can offer home office jobs for people who are caring for children or elderly relatives, and thus avoid the loss of knowledge and talent. Often global virtual teams work on projects in the matrix structure; however, it is more and more frequent that you have regular teams who are no longer co-located. For example, the team leader works from London, half of his team works in Poland, a quarter in Germany, and the rest in France. Many outsourcing projects have led to such team structures.

### Challenges

Due to cost reductions, the members of such teams often cannot meet face to face more than once a year. Most of the communication is therefore via telephone or other virtual communication. For many team members, the lack of body language signals makes collaboration difficult. Conflicts are often more difficult to resolve if you does not meet each other in person. It is also much more likely to misunderstand each other when you are only communicating in written form. On the one hand, facial expressions are lacking to clarify the meaning of a statement; on the other hand, it is more difficult to ask clarifying questions without appearing negative in a written conversation. The fact that these teams often consist of members of different cultures does not make it easier. There are often misunderstandings about agreements, deadlines and responsibilities. One problem that is mentioned most often when we are working with virtual teams is the lack of accountability – in other words, something that you promise someone that you are not likely to run across at the coffee machine does not seem to be as urgent as something you promise someone who you see every day.

In one of our seminars about "Global Virtual Teams," we ask members from different nations about their interpretation of the sentence: "You will get the report on Friday." The German participant said that it would be okay to get the report after lunch on Friday. This way she would be able to actually work on it before the end of business on Friday. For the French participant, the end of business on Friday around 6 p.m. would still be okay – he would then read the report on the weekend or on Monday morning. The Indian participant said that it would be okay for him to get the report at 10 o'clock local time on Monday. He would probably not be able to read the report much earlier anyway since on Monday morning he would have to answer the e-mails and calls from the weekend. The participants of the seminar were very surprised about the different assessments and laughed about the result. They concluded that they would specify exactly which result they needed from whom by when exactly (time and date) so that everyone knows what the expectations are and nobody is disappointed.

*For many team members, it is difficult to communicate without non-verbal clues like gestures and facial expressions.*

### *Why is a solution-focused approach especially useful for virtual teams?*

As we have already mentioned, solution-focus works without interpreting personal behavior. Instead, we look for clear descriptions of the desired future. This alone makes working in global virtual teams much easier. Instead of assuming that all Germans do not have a sense of humor, all Indians are unreliable, etc. and becoming angry when something does not happen the way we assumed it would happen, we simply assume that misunderstandings are normal. We therefore pick up the phone and clarify what we need differently. The general suspicion is turned into general acceptance. Studies of global virtual teams and intercultural collaboration show that trust, confidence, enthusiastic and appreciative communication, as well as a high tolerance for ambiguity, are essential for the success of global virtual teams. (Jarvenpaa & Leidner, 1999; Stahl, 2001.) solution-focus exemplifies the success factors to a high degree: in our experience, solution-focused teamwork and solution-focused team leadership are optimal for global virtual teams.

In principle, solution-focused coaching in virtual teams is no different than coaching co-located teams. The only difference is that most of the conversation will happen on the telephone, via video conference or in a virtual conference room.

The success factors for effective virtual meetings are similar to those of non-virtual meetings: There is an atmosphere of openness and understanding. The goals of the participants are known and are similar to one another. There is a relaxed and productive atmosphere. Everybody can talk and everybody is interested in a solution or further development of the topics. Problems are discussed constructively. There is only one difficulty in virtual meetings that you do not have in face-to-face meetings: in virtual meetings, you do not realize if somebody is doing something else parallel to the meeting; for example, writing an e-mail. Most platforms do not offer a solution for this. One exception is the German platform "vitero" (www.vitero.de). It is very important to make sure not to lose people in the meeting by keeping it interactive by asking questions.

We consciously plan our virtual coaching sessions to include moments in which everyone can participate. If there is anyone in the telephone conference who is not making the best use of his or her time, we do not see this as a personal criticism. Rather, we interpret this as the person's attempt at being efficient. If we know that somebody is not so interested in the topic of the training or conference, we can actively deal with it and avoid misunderstandings. For most teams, our way of dealing with this issue serves as a good example: we often ask people whether their participation in a telephone conference is still useful for them and what would possibly make it more useful? If we are talking about an issue that is not very relevant for one of the participants, we offer that person the opportunity to simply continue listening and do something else in the meantime. This way the participants can notice when the topic changes and come back to active participation when the topic turns to something more relevant to them. This possibility is not often used by virtual teams. People seem to fear that their conversation partners will interpret this kind of behavior as a lack of respect. If you start by giving everybody the benefit of the doubt this cannot happen. The calmer and friendlier person asks whether it is okay not to participate, the better for all involved. Compare: "This meeting is useless – I really have better things to do with my time" with "Okay, I think you are really managing this very well. At the moment I do not think I can really add anything. Would it be okay for you if I dial back in in half an hour or continue working on my presentation while I just listen?"

Example 24: **The virtual team**

Initial conversation

*I met the team leader of a global team in the IT industry at a confer-*
*ence about coaching. The team members were distributed over the*
*US, Germany, France, UK, and Singapore. This team was responsible*
*for the formation of the global marketing strategy. All team members*
*were managers themselves. They managed people who reported di-*
*rectly to them and also other people in the local marketing and sales*
*organizations who they were connected to via matrix structures. Ms.*
*Dupont was enthusiastic about the possibilities that SF work offers for*
*global teams and wanted us to coach her and her team. She was full*
*of praise for her team members, but thought that the coaching could*
*help team members to deal with some processes faster and smoother,*
*especially misunderstandings that could be clarified more quickly and in*
*a more natural way. Since each of her team members was also work-*
*ing in other global teams, together with local marketing units, team*
*coaching would also be useful for her team members in this context.*
*Ms. Dupont was very open and trusted us to elicit the goals of the*
*coaching from the team and did not want to mention too many of her*
*goals of the coaching. She really wanted to involve her team as much*
*as possible in finding out what could be improved.*

Team interviews

*Of course, she was enthusiastic about our suggestion to ask the team*
*members what was going well and what could still be better. I con-*
*ducted telephone conversations with all team members and led half-*
*open interviews with the following questions:*

- *What do you appreciate about your team?*
- *What do you have to get right as a team in the next year?*

- *Suppose I call you again after half a year and your team has developed in the direction that you desire – what will you be telling me about your team then?*

- *On a scale of 0 to 10, where 10 is that you have already reached that point (which means that no development is necessary) and 0 is the complete opposite, where do you see your team?*

- *Why is it X and not 0?*

- *What could be a next step in the direction of X+1?*

  *The team members were all proud of their team since they were cooperating really well in spite of the intercultural differences. They saw the design of the new global marketing strategy and good communication with local partners as the most important tasks for the next year. The team scale was between five and seven. Most team members mentioned as a next step that they would have to think about how to communicate the new strategy in the different countries together rather than doing it each by themselves. They had the feeling they would be able to learn a lot from each other. Best practice sharing usually did nott happen because everybody was always pressed for time; this was something that everybody wanted to do but it somehow it never happened. Most team members would also like to try out new forms of communication like a webinar or web-conferencing. Some wanted to find out more personal information about the other team members in order to better understand in which context other people live and work.*

Team coaching (online)
*We agreed on three dates with two hours each for the team coaching. These coachings took place at rotating times of the day: this way, not only one location bore the brunt of having to stay late or getting up early in the morning. However, since everybody was very enthusiastic, it was not a problem if the Americans would have to get up very early once and team members in Singapore had to stay late and phone in from home. We used WebEx as a communication platform. WebEx, like other platforms (for example GoToMeeting, ATT, open webinars,*

and dim dim) offer the possibility to share slides and use electronic surveys, or to write something on a slide and use it like a flip chart. Such joint activities are very useful to substitute the missing visual information. The three dates had different topics: the first meeting was about best practice sharing and communication strategy. In the second meeting, team members talked about getting to know and understand each other better. The last meeting happened a few weeks later and served to evaluate the results and to elicit further topics.

First meeting: Best Practice Sharing

I first clarified the goals of the session together with the participants: "What should be better after two hours?" "What needs to happen here to get there?" The participants jotted down their answers in the chat room of WebEx so I could get back to them at the end of the webinar. Participants primarily wanted to exchange which procedures and communications strategies worked in the discussion of the marketing strategy with the local marketing teams and what pitfalls should be avoided.

I then asked the participants to work in breakout rooms in mixed small groups (most conference lines today offer breakout rooms so that you can break up a larger group in a telephone conference into small groups just like you would when you are facilitating a face-to-face meeting). Within the groups, everyone was asked to share a story where communication had worked well in the last couple of weeks. They were also asked to take notes about what their contribution to that communication was. Afterwards, the whole group came back into the plenary and reported about the discussions. The results were summarized right there in a word document under the heading "What is already working – what should we do more of?"

The next question was who would notice if the communication with the local marketing teams improved? The participants said that team members in their local teams would notice, and customers would notice, as well. The customers would notice that there is a more unified *strategy which is still very customized for the local markets. Again the group went into the breakout rooms. One group talked about how team members from the local marketing teams would notice, the other group talked about how they would notice themselves, and the third group talked about how customers would notice. These results were then also discussed within the whole group. They summarized their ideas for implementation in the same Word document under the heading, "What can we do to improve the communication with the local marketing teams?" Later I heard that this word document had somewhat acquired a life of its own and was sent around the whole marketing group. This was very positive for everyone. At the end of the meeting we looked again at the goals that were set at the beginning of the meeting and realized that most of them had been reached.*

## Second meeting: Getting to know each other better

*The second meeting had the goal of getting to know each other better. To prepare for the meeting, we sent an e-mail and asked the partici-pants to write down their questions for the other team members. The team members answered with some serious, but also some funny, ques-tions. There were questions like, "How does your school system work?" and "Have you ever ridden an elephant?" and anything in between. From this selection of questions, we created a small questionnaire and asked everybody to answer those questions that he or she would like to answer. Everybody was asked to create one or two PowerPoint slides with their answers and include some personal pictures.*

*In the Web meeting, we asked everybody to pretend that we were having coffee together and explicitly mentioned in the invitation that everybody should bring their favorite nonalcoholic drink – coffee or tea – for the telephone conference. The meeting started with a small exercise. We asked the participants to think about one thing that they appreciate about each of the other participants, one thing that this person is doing that is useful for the team. They were then asked to share that observation with the respective person in the private chat* room. Afterwards, the participants presented their sides and there was a lot of laughter and fun. People had the possibility to ask questions and explain about their personal life as much as they felt comfortable. After the meeting, the team felt they had actually found out something important about the other team members and felt much more comfortable and closer to each other, even though they had not been able to see each other face-to-face.

Third Meeting: Follow-up

The third meeting started with the question: "What's better?" We wrote down the results on a PowerPoint slide. I then asked again what the team would have to get right in the next three months. This question was again answered by small groups in breakout rooms. Three points emerged. I wrote them down as scales on a PowerPoint slide:

Collaboration with local organizations
0----------------------------------------------10

Understanding each other and taking time to develop team spirit
0----------------------------------------------10

Dealing with misunderstandings
0----------------------------------------------10

The team agreed to scale these parameters individually and talk about them once a month in their weekly team call. They would then talk about what is going well and what could be the next step. Finally, I asked the team to listen to my observations about the team. I talked about what makes me confident that the team will reach their goals and about what I had observed that was already going in the desired direction.

The team had become accustomed to using the WebEx meeting platform through these three team coachings and started using the technology for many of their calls. We later got the feedback that working in small groups in the larger team call was very efficient and that they *continued using breakout rooms in their calls. We will have another review meeting in half the year where we asked, "What is better?" and "What are some of the things you have to get right in the next half year?"*

# Summary

Conflict

- Basics
- Steps of conflict mediation
  - Establishing and maintaining a good working relationship
  - Goal – goal behind the goal
  - Exceptions and resources
  - Next steps
  - Experiments
  - Agreement and actions
- Bullying / Mobbing
  - Prevention of bullying
  - Concrete allegations of bullying
- Teambuilding
  - Situations
  - Structure
    - Clarifying the contract
    - Interviews
    - Workshop
- Getting-to-know-each-other-bingo
- Mixed interviews
- Resource board
- Fun activities
- What do we want to keep

- Criteria of good task assignment and distribution
  - Follow up
- Virtual teams
  - What are global virtual teams?
  - Challenges
  - Why is a solution-focused approach especially useful for virtual teams?

# Postscript

Everything you never wanted to know about team coaching and were afraid to ask! I hope many of your questions on solution-focused team coaching have been answered. If not, please look at our website or read our blog. We are also always happy to answer any questions that you might have: www.solutionsacademy.com

More publications can be found on our publishing house website: www.solutionsacademy.info

# References

Andersen, T. (1991): *The reflecting team: Dialogues and dialogues about the dialogues* (1st). New York: Norton.

Bannink, F. (2009): *Praxis der Lösungs-fokussierten Mediation: Konzepte, Methoden und Übungen für MediatorInnen und Führungskräfte* (1st ed.). Stuttgart: Concadora-Verl.

Bannink, F. (2010): *Handbook of solution focused conflict management*. Toronto: Hogrefe.

Belbin, R. M. (1981): *Management teams. Why they succeed or fail.* New York: Wiley.

Bonsen, M. zur & Maleh, C. (2001): *Appreciative Inquiry (AI) – Der Weg zu Spitzenleistungen*, Weinheim und Basel: Beltz Verlag.

Briggs Myers, I. & McCaulley, M. H. (1992): *Manual, a guide to the development and use of the Myers-Briggs type indicator.* Palo Alto, Calif.: Consulting Psychologists Press.

Cauffman, L., & Dierolf, K. (2006). *The solution tango: Seven simple steps to solutions in management.* London: Marshall Cavendish Limited; Cyan Communications Limited.

Dolan, Y. (1991): *Resolving Sexual Abuse.* New York: Norton.

Furman, B. & Ahola, T. (2004): *Twin Star: Lösungen vom andern Stern.* Heidelberg: Carl Auer.

Furman B. & Ahola, T. (2007): *Change through Cooperation: Handbook of reteaming.* Helsinki: Helsinki Brief Therapy Institute, Inc.

Furman, B. & Ahola, T. (2010): *Es ist nie zu spät, erfolgreich zu sein: Ein lösungsfokussiertes Programm für Coaching von Organisationen, Teams und Einzelpersonen; [Coaching – Beratung]* (1st ed.). Heidelberg: Carl Auer Verl.

Geisbauer, W. (Ed.). (2006): *Reteaming: Methodenhandbuch zur lösungsorientierten Beratung* (2nd ed.). Heidelberg: Carl Auer Verl.

Gay, F. (1999): *DISG-Persönlichkeits-Profil. Mit dem original DISG-Testmaterial zur Selbstauswertung [Verstehen Sie sich selbst besser; Schöpfen Sie Ihre Möglichkeit aus; Entdecken Sie Ihre Stärken und Schwächen].* 13. Aufl. Offenbach: GABAL.

Jackson, P. Z. & McKergow, M. (2002): *The solutions focus. The simple way to positive change.* London: Nicholas Brealey.

Jarvenpaa, S. & Leidner, D. E. (1999): *Communication and Trust in Global Virtual Teams* In: Organization Science 10, S. 791–815.

DeJong, P. &. B. I. (1998). *Interviewing for solutions.* Thomson: Brooks/Cole.

Kim, J. S. (2008): *Examining the effectiveness of solution-focused brief therapy: A meta-analysis.* Research on Social Work Practice 18: 107–116.

Meier, D. (2005). *Team Coaching with the Solutioncircle: A Practical Guide to Solutions Focused Team Development.* Cheltenham: Solutions Books.

Ramseyer, F. &. T. W. (op. 2008): *Synchrony in Dyadic Psychotherapy Sessions.* In: S. Vrobel, O. E. Rössler, & T. Marks-Tarlow (Eds.), *Simultaneity* (pp. 329–348). Hackensack, NJ: World Scientific.

Rohrig, P., & Clarke, J. (2008). *57 SF activities for facilitators and consultants: Putting solutions focus into action.* Cheltenham: Solutions Books.

Shazer, S. de (1988): *Clues. Investigating solutions in brief therapy.* 1st. New York: W. W. Norton.

Shazer, S. de (1997): *Some thoughts on language use in therapy.* In: Contemporary Family Therapy 19 (133–141).

Shazer, S. de, Dolan, Y. M., & Korman, H. (2007). *More than miracles: The state of the art of solution-focused brief therapy.* New York: Haworth Press.

Shazer, S. de & Berg, I.K. (1997): *Together, in the middle of the bed.* Brief treatment of a couple. Milwaukee, Wis.: Brief Family Therapy Center.

Stahl, G.K. (2001): *Internationaler Einsatz von Führungskräften. Probleme, Bewältigung, Erfolg.* In: Ulrich Krystek (Hg.): *Handbuch Internationalisierung. Eine Herausforderung für die Unternehmensführung.* 2., völlig neu bearb. u. erw. Berlin: Springer, S. 277–301.

Tuckman, B. W. (1965): *Developmental sequence in small groups.* In: Psychological Bulletin 63 (6), S. 384–399.

Varga Kibéd, M. von & Sparrer, I. (2005): *Ganz im Gegenteil: Tetralemmaarbeit und andere Grundformen systemischer Strukturaufstellungen – für Querdenker und solche, die es werden wollen* (5., überarb). Heidelberg: Carl Auer Systeme.

Vrobel, S., Rössler, O. E., & Marks-Tarlow, T. (op. 2008): *Simultaneity.* Hackensack, NJ: World Scientific.

Young, S. (2009): *Solution Focused Schools: Anti-Bullying and Beyond.* London: BT Press.

Ziegler, P. & Hiller, T. (2001): *Recreating partnership. A solution-oriented, collaborative approach to couples therapy.* New York, London: Norton.

## Webressources:

http://www.insights-group.de 26.5.2011

http://www.myersbriggs.org 26.5.2011

http://www.vitero.de/deutsch/home/ 16.3.2011

http://www.gotomeeting.de 16.3.2011

http://www.webex.com/ 16.3.2011

http://www.openwebinars.com/ 16.3.2011

http://www.dimdim.com/ 16.3.2011

http://solutionfocusedchange.blogspot.com/2007/10/who-invented-miracle-question.html 6.2.2012

Reich, K. (Hg.): Methodenpool. In: URL: http://methodenpool.uni-koeln.de 28.11.2012

http://www.agilimanifesto.org 13.02.2013

# Index

Active listening   45

Agile   11, 15, 27, 132

Agreements and actions   162, 163, 174

Ahola, Tapani   15, 17, 28, 84, 116, 120, 122–130, 164

Analysis of the problem   25, 28, 31, 33, 46, 47, 90, 123

Aquarium   151

Bannink, Fredrike   17, 158

Basics   15ff

Bullying   11, 16, 165–169

Clarifying the contract   25–28, 50, 78, 83, 96–111, 115, 117, 170

Columbo method   146-147

Communication   20, 28, 54, 55, 56, 102, 112, 113, 115, 121, 132, 138, 142, 159, 166, 174, 175, 178, 179, 180

Complexity   25, 35

Confidence   23, 31, 36-38, 45, 46, 50, 58, 65, 76, 81-83, 95, 98,106, 107, 110, 112, 114, 116, 130, 141, 148, 149, 159, 160, 161,163, 175

Conflict   16, 33, 39, 42, 45, 48, 55, 56, 89, 113, 114, 126, 144–173

Coping question   22, 58-63, 147

Culture   23, 49, 53, 77, 84, 129, 146, 159, 174

Decision making   30, 41, 72, 77, 78, 87, 89, 95, 98, 100, 118, 131, 132, 133, 135

De-escalation   164

Drawing a picture   58, 71, 75

Endless chatter   150-151

Exceptions and resources   32–35, 41, 43, 47, 66–67, 90, 95, 99, 102, 110, 153, 155, 160

Experiments   23, 25, 27, 44, 57, 84, 161

Flipchart   37, 40, 50, 52, 55-66, 67, 73, 74, 75, 78, 80, 85, 87, 88, 94

Follow-up   25, 26, 65, 69, 71, 77, 90, 115, 116, 120, 132, 173, 181

Furman, Ben   15, 17, 28, 84, 116, 120, 122–130, 164

Goal setting   53-58

Grammar   46, 97, 98

Humming   66

Incremental approach   27

Individual coaching   15, 23, 25, 31, 33, 39, 40–48, 50, 58, 77, 91, 115, 117

Individual work   52, 73, 94, 151

Interviews   26, 27, 43, 58, 80, 106–109, 115, 116, 140, 167, 168, 170, 171, 177

Kim Berg, Insoo   12, 17, 33, 44, 62, 68, 70, 141, 153

Leadership   27, 30, 33, 101, 102, 103, 106, 107, 113, 126, 130, 153, 175

Letter from the future   57, 58

Listening   40–47, 61, 84, 176

Maori method   159

Meier, Daniel   12, 13, 15, 17, 24, 27, 117–119

Miracle board   75

Miracle question    58, 68–77, 90, 95, 120, 125

Multipartiality    42, 43, 44, 47, 51

Negative participants    137, 154

Paradoxical silence    152

Personal superlative    50

Phase models    19

Pinboard timeline    95

Plenary discussion    50, 51, 55, 56, 58, 60, 66, 72, 73, 74, 83, 116, 118, 119, 140, 171, 179

Positive paranoia    84, 95

Pretend feedback round    57

Raising hands    66

Resource board    171

Resource gossip    84, 95

Reteaming    12, 15, 116, 117, 120, 123

Röhrig, Peter    4, 12, 52, 53

Role play    75, 75, 91, 152, 164

Scaling Walk    63, 64, 65, 66, 189, 190

Scaling    27, 61, 62, 63-75, 81 ,83, 94, 95, 116, 119, 134, 160, 166

Shazer, Steve de    12, 17,  22, 23, 32, 39, 40, 41, 44, 45, 55, 62, 68, 71

Small groups    24, 51, 53, 59, 60, 61, 63, 65, 66, 67, 72, 73, 74, 75, 86, 94, 95, 111, 116, 118, 119, 134, 135, 151, 152, 164, 179, 181

Small steps    25, 27, 33, 47, 77, 79, 90, 95, 99, 119

Solution onion    52

SolutionCircle    12, 15, 117, 119

Sparrer, Insa    4, 13, 87

Strong emotions    152–154

Teambuilding    16, 169–173

Tenets    18–20, 47, 96

Tetralemma    87

Tools    48–94

Trust    39, 46, 111, 114, 117, 170, 175

Varga von Kibéd, Matthias    4, 13, 87

Virtual teams    173–181

What is better    50–52, 71, 73, 94, 115, 116, 159, 173, 182

Working relationship    40–41, 48–50, 89, 94, 149, 153, 159, 161, 182

# List of Examples

Example 1:     Automatic travel expenses . . . . . . . . . . . . . . . . . . . . . . . . . . . . .     21

Example 2:     The problem on the table  . . . . . . . . . . . . . . . . . . . . . . . . . . . . .     23

Example 3:     The dominant boss – the disempowered team leader  . . . . . . . .     29

Example 4:     The team scale  . . . . . . . . . . . . . . . . . . . . . . . . . . . . . . . . . . . .     34

Example 5:     The initiative for excellence that backfired  . . . . . . . . . . . . . . .     36

Example 6:     More or less communication?  . . . . . . . . . . . . . . . . . . . . . . . . .     56

Example 7:     Scaling walk in training situations . . . . . . . . . . . . . . . . . . . . . .     64

Example 8:     Strategy meeting  . . . . . . . . . . . . . . . . . . . . . . . . . . . . . . . . . . .     71

Example 9:     The Russian countess . . . . . . . . . . . . . . . . . . . . . . . . . . . . . . . .     72

Example 10:    A useless presentation coaching . . . . . . . . . . . . . . . . . . . . . . . .     82

Example 11:    Welcome to the jungle  . . . . . . . . . . . . . . . . . . . . . . . . . . . . . . .     93

Example 12:    But where is your feedback?  . . . . . . . . . . . . . . . . . . . . . . . . . . .     101

Example 13:    A second chance . . . . . . . . . . . . . . . . . . . . . . . . . . . . . . . . . . . .     106

Example 14:    An anonymized report . . . . . . . . . . . . . . . . . . . . . . . . . . . . . . . .     110

Example 15      . . . . . . . . . . . . . . . . . . . . . . . . . . . . . . . . . . . . . . . . . . . . . . . .     131

Example 16      . . . . . . . . . . . . . . . . . . . . . . . . . . . . . . . . . . . . . . . . . . . . . . . .     131

Example 17      . . . . . . . . . . . . . . . . . . . . . . . . . . . . . . . . . . . . . . . . . . . . . . . .     131

Example 18:    The negative engineer . . . . . . . . . . . . . . . . . . . . . . . . . . . . . . . .     138

Example 19:    Yet another change!  . . . . . . . . . . . . . . . . . . . . . . . . . . . . . . . . .     140

Example 20:    The coach as idiot . . . . . . . . . . . . . . . . . . . . . . . . . . . . . . . . . . .     144

Example 21:    Anger and frustration . . . . . . . . . . . . . . . . . . . . . . . . . . . . . . . .     153

Example 22:    It's not that life's a piece of cake . . . . . . . . . . . . . . . . . . . . . . . .     156

Example 23:    The files are in a mess . . . . . . . . . . . . . . . . . . . . . . . . . . . . . . . .     162

Example 24:    The virtual team . . . . . . . . . . . . . . . . . . . . . . . . . . . . . . . . . . . . .     177

# List of Exercises

Exercise 1:   Practicing escalation . . . . . . . . . . . . . . . . . . . . . . . . . . . . . .   30

Exercise 2:   Multipartiality . . . . . . . . . . . . . . . . . . . . . . . . . . . . . . . . . . .   44

Exercise 3:   "Together in the middle of the bed" . . . . . . . . . . . . . . . . . . . .   44

Exercise 4:   Listening . . . . . . . . . . . . . . . . . . . . . . . . . . . . . . . . . . . . . . .   45

Exercise 5:   Goal setting . . . . . . . . . . . . . . . . . . . . . . . . . . . . . . . . . . . . .   54

Exercise 6:   Scaling walk for self-coaching . . . . . . . . . . . . . . . . . . . . . . . .   64

Exercise 7:   Eau de collègue . . . . . . . . . . . . . . . . . . . . . . . . . . . . . . . . . .   126

Exercise 8:   Giving and taking criticism . . . . . . . . . . . . . . . . . . . . . . . . . .   130

Exercise 9:   The coach as idiot . . . . . . . . . . . . . . . . . . . . . . . . . . . . . . . . .   144

Exercise 10:  We have ways of making you talk . . . . . . . . . . . . . . . . . . . . . .   151

Exercise 11:  De-escalation . . . . . . . . . . . . . . . . . . . . . . . . . . . . . . . . . . . .   164

# Kirsten Dierolf M.A.

Kirsten leads intelligent conversations with great people: pragmatic, solution-focused and 100% bullshit free. She has been working as executive and team coach, organizational and talent developer since 1996 mainly for global corporations in finance, IT and the pharmaceutical industry.

Kirsten is founder and manager of "SolutionsAcademy" an international consulting firm and publishing house specializing in solution-focus practice in organisations. Her work never revolves around analyzing root causes or identifying who is to blame or classifications of any sort. Her consistent focus is on the goals and resources of her clients and the first steps toward reaching a desired future. This way, Kirsten is able to help move the trickiest situations forward in the most complex and difficult environments.

Kirsten has worked in across Europe, North and South America, Africa, Asia and Australia (the penguins are still missing). She enjoys public speaking and has given many keynotes on almost all continents. She teaches in the "Master of Supervision" program at the protestant university of applied science in Freiburg.

Kirsten is "EU-ambassador for female entrepreneurship", a title awarded by the European Commission, and president of SFCT, the association for the quality development of solution-focused consulting and training.

Liselotte Baeijaert und
Anton Stellamans

# Resilienz:
# Ein Werkstattbuch
# zur Widerstandskraft

Aus dem Englischen von
Jutta Bleuel und
Kirsten Dierolf

ISBN: 978-3-944293-01-1

140 S., Paperback, € 24,95